# CLASSICAL BUJUTSU

# CLASSICAL
# BUJUTSU

---

## THE MARTIAL ARTS
## AND WAYS OF JAPAN

---

### VOLUME ONE

DONN F. DRAEGER

WEATHERHILL
NEW YORK & TOKYO

TITLE PAGE: Woodblock print by Yoshie Chikanobu showing Nitta Yoshisada, a fourteenth-century warrior, blocking arrows (*yadome*).

TEXT DECORATIONS AND ILLUSTRATIONS: Drawings of warriors' equipment from Yamawaki Shojun's *Buki Hyaku Zu* (Drawings of Warriors' Equipment), published in 1848; drawings of warriors from Katsushika Hokusai's *Gempei Meigashira E-hon Musha Bunrui* (An Illustrated Catalogue of Various Warriors of the Minamoto and Taira Clans), published in 1841, and from E. Papinot's *Historical and Geographical Dictionary of Japan*, published in 1910. All photographs, except where credit is given, are by the author.

First edition, 1973
First paperback edition, 1990
Fourth printing, 2000

Published by Weatherhill, Inc.
41 Monroe Turnpike
Trumbull, CT 06611

Draeger, Donn F.
    Classical bujutsu / Donn F. Draeger.
        p.   cm.
    Originally published: 1973. (The martial arts and ways of Japan; v. 1)
    Includes index.
    ISBN 0-8348-0233-3 (softcover)
    1. Military art and science—Japan—History.
    2. Weapons—Japan—History.  I. Title II. Series—Martial arts and ways of Japan; v. 1.
U43.J3D7  1996
355'.00952—dc20                                        95-48459
                                                            CIP

# Contents

That we may these virgin forms
yet a little while detain . . .

YOSHIMINE MUNESADA

# Part One

# THE COMBATIVE
# RATIONALE

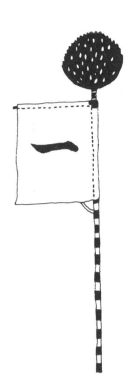

CHAPTER ONE

# JAPAN'S MARTIAL TRADITION

Civilization begins, because the beginning of
civilization is a military advantage.

Walter Bagehot

The processes of change have been so great during the past few
decades that in many ways they threaten to leave us poorer instead
of richer so far as our knowledge of traditional institutions is
concerned. That is why even if the more ambitious and thorough
aims of scholarly investigation are only indirectly served, it is
important that a book like this be written describing a greatly mis-
understood segment of old Japanese society, one that was a veritable
institution. Much of the total culture that is characteristic of Japan
was influenced by that institution, and therefore this book is its own
justification.

Though no particular class of the Japanese nation had a monopoly
on *Yamato-damashii,* "Japanese spirit," there was perhaps no segment
of Japanese society so filled with stirring displays of this spirit as the
warrior class. A study of how some of these displays were inspired
may lead us to a fuller understanding of what has made Japan what
it was in the past, what it is now, and what it will be in the future.

This book contains a specialized account of the classical Japanese
warrior. Writers living in the ease of eras following those during
which the classical warrior actually flourished used ideal themes in
their writings, themes eulogizing such attributes of these warriors
as loyalty, honor, courage, self-reliance, self-sacrifice, obedience, and

disdain for remuneration for services performed. To be sure, the historical annals are filled with illustrations of these admirable qualities, and it would be grossly unfair to suggest that such a code of warrior ethics was honored more in the breach than the observance; but the fact remains that flagrant abuses kept that code from having a universal warranty. My intention in this book is only to provide a small chink in the armor of time, through which the reader may gain a substantially less emotional view of the classical Japanese warrior than heretofore presented.

Because this book is not intended to be a definitive work, the tedious accounts of warfare that abound in military histories have been expunged except for such references as are vital to a description of the Japanese martial ethos. Moreover, the abstruse philosophical speculations that are often overused by writers to buttress their descriptions of the warrior's martial appetite have been eschewed, since the primary purpose of this book is to provide an insight into the technical fabric of the classical warrior's martial culture—the components of his actual skill at arms, his fighting arts. These are known as the *bujutsu,* or martial arts.

Belisarius, the Roman emperor Justinian's outstanding cavalry general, noted that "the first blessing is peace, as is agreed upon by all men who have even a small share of reason." Yet history is a path of blood, and it would seem that if combat were to become impossible, or if it became a lost art, man would have to rediscover it in order to redeem his life from a course of boredom and degradation. For whether we agree with Jean-Jacques Rousseau that war and civilization had a common origin or with Friedrich Nietzsche that war is "an ennobling experience for a society as a whole," or prefer Arnold Toynbee's thesis that wars act as the "proximate causes" that tend to destroy every civilization, it is impossible to disregard man's willingness to fight against his fellow man.

No clear-cut, satisfactory answer has ever been given as to why men wage combat. Men have been fighting creatures and have engaged in destroying each other ever since they first came into conflict in the prehistoric past. Whether man's desire to fight stems from human nature or is the child of civilization, it is abundantly clear that fighting is a behavioral pattern from which he has been

*Three types of arrow*

*Missile weapons*

unable to free himself. It appears that Pliny the Elder was right when he wrote that the "only tearful animal, man, through the nature of his being, is destined to a life of warfare."

Some consider man's pugnacity as an instinct that no amount of cultural conditioning will overcome. Others suppose it to be the result of environmental pressures that force men into conflict with one another. In either case, it is difficult to find fault with Thomas Hobbes, for whom man's "only social relation was a state of war." About all that can be safely said, unremarkable as it may be, is that combat manifests the existence of life and that the rudiments for fighting lie dormant in every man until the right stimuli are applied.

Man in all ages has shown a great aptitude for devising instruments for and methods of combat; no race is so primitive as to have no weapons. Weapons and methods of combat existed before nations evolved, and nations were not long in existence before warfare was used as an instrument of national policy and justified by reasons of state, however the latter were rationalized in universal terms of justice, authority, or evolutionary utility. And so there is no modern state that does not possess a martial tradition intimately related to its very existence.

Haniwa *warrior*

Martial tradition occupies an especially conspicuous place in the history and culture of Japan. Ancient *haniwa* grave figurines indicate a warrior culture and spirit. Shinto mythology tells of the forcible unification of Japan by the imperial clan. The earliest extant forms of literature, the eighth-century *Kojiki* (Record of Ancient Matters), *Nihon Shoki* (Chronicles of Japan), *Kogoshui* (Record of Ancient History), and *Man'yoshu* (Collection of Myriad Leaves) all contain references to an early warrior culture. In the *Man'yoshu*, an anthology of poems, we find reference to the *masurao*, the fighting man of courage: *"Masurao no kiyoki sono na."* This infers that the honor of the warrior must be unstained, through the elevation of duties above rights, and that bravery is an aspect of loyalty.

The sentiments of this early period eventually lost their impact as ethical matters for the individual conscience and became instead only conventions that lingered on as ideals; they were exalted in literature of the Kamakura period (1185–1336): the *Hogen Monogatari* (Tale of the Hogen War), *Heiji Monogatari* (Tale of the Heiji War), *Heike*

*Archer*

*Monogatari* (Tale of the House of Taira), *Gempei Seisuiki* (Record of the Rise and Fall of the Minamoto and the Taira), and *Azuma Kagami* (Mirror of the Eastland).

Any careful examination of early Japanese literature, especially of the above-mentioned *gunki monogatari,* or military romances, will reveal an important fact: despite the bias of such literature toward giving a favorable impression of the warrior class, examples of disloyalty, cowardice, treachery, and self-interest predominate over those of higher qualities, indicating how bad the actual conditions of the warrior's life were.

It is doubtful whether the Japanese people and the country as a whole can really be understood or appreciated by anyone without a degree of knowledge of their martial culture. At the same time, it is doubtful whether the Japanese can be accused of engaging in what anthropologists refer to as "ritual warfare." This term refers to the custom of certain peoples who regard war as being more than just a necessary evil. For these peoples, peace means the stagnation of their societies and their eventual destruction. By ritual warfare is meant the regular repetition of warfare, and thus its indispensability. Ordinary warfare is rationalized differently, being a profane rather than a sacred matter, as is ritual warfare. However, in order that ritual warfare may be considered a legitimate institution, it must

*Wooden saddletrees*

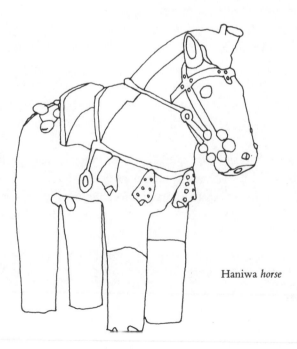

Haniwa *horse*

stem from prehistoric custom. The evidence we have of conditions in prehistoric Japan gives no clue as to whether the earliest settlers of the Japanese islands were excessively warlike or were engaged in warfare on the scale required to make it of the ritual type. Moreover, physical anthropologists, such as Maurice Davie, find the yellow race to be only moderately warlike, far less so than either the white or the black race.

Yet it is undeniable that the early Japanese had a penchant for martial prowess. They appear to have arrived at an understanding of combative activities quite apart from the context assigned by many other peoples, waxing metaphysical over them as contemplative disciplines. Even by the time the Japanese had devoted much of their energy to making standardized weapons of steel, by the eighth or ninth century A.D., no technical records are extant that indicate that systematic methods of training warriors for combat had been developed. It is only with the rise of the classical warrior to political power, in the twelfth century, that the Japanese began to exhibit what might be termed an inclination for ritual warfare.

*Armored faceplate and tail cover for a horse*

Interpreters of Japanese history often fail to distinguish between the classical warrior and the modern soldier. Indeed, many modern Japanese have been taught and believe that the fighting man of their age represents a precise continuation of the warrior spirit of the past. This lamentable state of affairs represents the view of people who judge matters from the evidence of isolated cases, make arbitrary generalizations, and have only a superficial knowledge of Japanese martial culture. Thus a secondary purpose of this book is to demonstrate that there is a substantial difference between the classical Japanese warrior and his modern counterpart, the soldier.

Though the martial history of Japan covers approximately two millennia, it is for only a very small part of this time that classical warriors were functioning as a vigorous institution constant in style. Just how fragile was this moment of existence becomes clear after a careful study of Japanese history; and it is precisely because of this thin margin of time that historians and other writers are prone to gloss over this unique institution. By supposing that all Japanese fighting men formed a single group united by common principles and ideals it is very easy to ignore the fact that throughout Japanese history, men of combat have stemmed from different social strata, entered military service for different reasons, utilized different weapons (and thus different fighting techniques, strategies, and tactics), been guided by dissimilar ethics, enjoyed different rights and privileges, and exercised different political positions. Because these are group differences, they are not to be ignored. And in the interest of accuracy, they must not be lumped together under broad generalizations.

The word *bushi* is a generic term for the Japanese warrior; however, not all Japanese fighting men can correctly be called bushi. This term is most accurately used to describe the aristocratic warrior of protofeudal and feudal Japan, from the ninth to the nineteenth century. But even within that span of time there were fighting men who did not qualify for the appellation of bushi: the conscript soldiers of Oda Nobunaga and Toyotomi Hideyoshi in the sixteenth century are but two examples. Then, too, the bushi of the mid-to-late Tokugawa period (1603–1868), who were unskilled in combative arts though bushi by birthright, did not deserve the title on the basis of either their martial or their ethical qualities.

There were also many levels, or ranks, of bushi, which depended on the warrior's social status, his martial merit, and his position of precedence for the shogun's favor. The samurai was only one such rank, and by no means the highest. Originally, in pre-Kamakura times, the term samurai referred to servants who waited on the nobility. About the only connection any of these people had with a martial environment was the fact that they usually congregated around the guardhouses where fighting men were billeted to await orders from their superiors. Even when the term came to be generally extended to a certain kind of warrior, probably in the fourteenth century, the connotation of "service" was not completely removed. Because of this limiting background it is an error to refer to all warriors as samurai or to assume that the samurai, as a group, ruled the nation of Japan either during its periods of military government or at any other time.

Thus an accurate definition of the classical warrior is a complicated matter. This special institution does not easily submit to being defined precisely. Nevertheless, because we are specifically limited

*Ancient warrior*

in this book to a discussion of the classical warrior, in terms of his weapons and fighting arts, we are obliged to define what we mean by the term. The classical warrior is, simply, that type of fighting man who flourished under the martial discipline of Minamoto Yoritomo's *bakufu*, or military government, established at Kamakura in the late twelfth century. This was the first government recorded in Japanese history that was staffed almost entirely by professional warriors. After the demise of Yoritomo in 1199, the dominance of the Minamoto family in martial matters deteriorated, and the whole social, economic, and political complexion of the nation changed.

Partly because the emphasis in loyalty was shifted from the personal basis demanded by Yoritomo to an institutional one, the classical warrior saw his position of absolute authority give way to a new brand of mixed civil and military leadership. A different type of fighting man soon came to the fore; he was characterized by the worst examples of treachery, treason, anarchy, avarice, and general corruption Japan has ever known.

Nevertheless, we cannot simply tear off a portion of the calendar of history and use that cleanly torn section of chronology to help identify the classical warrior. To do so would be to infer, falsely, that no fighting men who operated before or after that time were classical warriors. The classical warriors of Yoritomo's time were men of moral weight, the most contained and least frivolous of Japanese men of combat. Their inspiring deeds, as they followed their destinies, altered the course of Japanese history. It is little wonder, then, that these forceful warriors very quickly became that

Tsuba, *swordguards*

*Crest of Kusunoki
Masashige*

type accepted as the traditional model of martial élan and virtue for all Japanese fighting men of later periods; that is, for those who respected this tradition and followed it in spite of social and economic pressures working against them. Except for some individual warriors, of whom the fourteenth-century hero Kusunoki Masashige is perhaps the outstanding example, and their closely knit bands of followers, the period between the thirteenth and seventeenth centuries saw the disunity of classical warriors. The possibility of using them as an effective force was reduced through their being distributed among fighting men of lesser clay. In the confusion that was produced in state machinery that had been greatly weakened by disputing factions, the reins of government finally fell to those who broke the classical warriors on their own blood and halted their blades by the "villainous saltpeter" of gunpowder. A military revolution was afoot.

Except possibly during the earliest years of the Tokugawa bakufu (1603–1868), that government was a military one in name only. More than two centuries of Tokugawa-contrived seclusion from foreign influences sounded the death knell for the classical warrior. A combination of civil authorities and of warriors who were disenchanted with the classical martial tradition recast the machinery of government, and finally, in the latter part of the nineteenth century, when the classical warrior and his purpose in society became an anachronism, he was swept into oblivion like the *condottiere* of Renaissance Italy. He was readily replaced by the citizen-soldiers of a conscript army in which the classical-warrior type was exceedingly rare.

Yet we must realize that the classical warrior, as a type, existed both before and after Yoritomo's time, though certainly not as the absolute ruling class of the land. In fact, the classical-warrior type exists even now.

Another important purpose of this book is to point up the carelessness of those who describe all Japanese martial skills under one classification, referring to the aggregate simply as "martial arts." Readers will notice the complete lack of mention in this book of such internationally known disciplines as judo, karate-do, aiki-do, and kendo. In fact, none of the so-called *do* forms finds a place in

*Part of a Tenshin Shoden Katori Shinto Ryu scroll showing Marishiten, guardian
deity of warriors, flanked by two other deities.*

this book. The omission is deliberate. There are very great differences
between the *bujutsu*, or martial arts, and the *budo*, or martial ways.
The bujutsu are combative systems designed by and for warriors to
promote self-protection and group solidarity. The budo are spiritual systems, not necessarily designed by warriors or for warriors,
for self-perfection of the individual. Since the latter were not
developed during the period in which the classical warrior functioned as the leader of an effective political and social ruling institution, the budo are outside the scope of this book and will be dealt
with in a subsequent volume. The reader should recognize the basic
difference between these two broad classifications of martial entities;
otherwise it will be impossible to understand clearly that part of
Japanese culture concerned with martial matters.

It is difficult to convey by any medium the essential nature of the
classical warrior's bujutsu, which he developed and used during the
period of his greatest martial activity. This is true partly because we
are so remote from that feudal era, but also because we are apt to
depend on sources that have little or no connection with the realities
of the classical warrior's life.

There is no dearth of information about the classical warrior,
but much of what has been recorded, as well as information passed
on by oral tradition, thrives on notoriously adumbrated history and
deliberately manipulated facts. Some of what stands for "history"

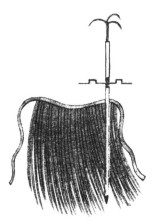

*Ceremonial apron
and helmet stand*

was written in peacetime by scholars who, because the best sources were not available to them, could not arrive at accurate conclusions. Military history, and to a lesser degree any form of art that depicts warriors, can be particularly unreliable. Some military history, as well as some art, is created to preserve reputations, to guard against the loss of secrets or the betrayal of weaknesses, and always with a possible future war in mind.

It is usual for advocates of martial cultures, apologists for the bushi in particular, to recall past glories in hyperbolic language. Working with more zeal than discrimination, they dwell at great length on what is martially courageous, loyal, disciplined, or skillfully performed. The battlefield virtues of the many are collectively transferred to the few in an attempt to enshrine national heroes. Severe critics of martial cultures work industriously to destroy such monuments to glory. They set forth facts and relationships that depict the bushi as men of insensibility who joy in human suffering or as crazed symbols of barbarism and cruelty. Equally damaging to the truth about the bushi are the evaluations of scholars who describe the bushi only in terms that appeal to the aesthetic sense; they succeed in taking the attention of their audience away from all but the good or the beautiful.

None of these lapidary positions is fair. It is most important, in the face of such overwhelmingly biased reporting, to demand intellectual honesty. We must try to see the bushi as they actually were and not make them out to be what we believe they ought to have been. The bushi were human, not superhuman. Though they were definitely supernormal as warriors, they also had faults and foibles, the limitations possessed by ordinary men, which were only to some degree offset by the workings of their *shugyo,* or austere discipline. And so we must take care to select only sources that show the least distortion of reality. The method I have chosen in this book depends essentially on special photographs. I believe it to be a reliable one, and through it the reader will be able to study the classical warriors and see them in some clarity and depth.

One of the best primary sources for our purpose, if critically used, is the martial *ryu.* There is no single word in the English language that can correctly and adequately describe the meaning of this term,

*Armor armlet*

but for convenience the ryu may be thought of as approximating a martial tradition. The ryu is, in fact, a corporate body, perpetuated by a line of lineal or collateral (*sei*) or nonconsanguineous (*dai*) headmasters.

To understand the ryu fully, the reader must think of it as possessing a personality of its own that subsumes those of the actual individuals who comprise the ryu. The ryu "lives" and "breathes," as well as "takes action," much as does a sentient being, but the full manifestation of its power lies well beyond the ken of man. The establishment of a ryu is always attributed to divine guidance (*tenshin sho*) that is bestowed upon its founder (*shosei* or *shodai*), and so elements of mysticism and the supernatural pervade all ryu. All founders of ryu, notwithstanding divine guidance, were warriors and martial geniuses who, after undergoing arduous discipline, experienced the flash of inspiration that led them to devise the technical characteristics of their ryu. The teachings of the ryu have the peculiarity of disclosing their essence only to those who have shown themselves worthy of the crucial experiences embodied in those teachings. And, because each ryu is made possible by the grace of divine guidance, it and its membership are protected by divine power that works through the medium of an oracle at a Shinto shrine.

Some nine thousand different martial ryu have been catalogued, but not all are extant. Unfortunately, no reliable documents of or about the protofeudal ryu (that is, those existing prior to the fourteenth century) have been discovered, and we must therefore depend only on those of the feudal era. Nor did all of these ryu align themselves with either of the governments, the imperial court or the bakufu—the military-based administrative government; therefore the martial strengths of such ryu are difficult to evaluate. Still other ryu, founded after the feudal age ended, are of no consequence for our study and are ignored, because classical warriors no longer existed as an influential force. In addition, I have selected from the feudal ryu only those that I believe to be technically the least changed from what they were at the peak of their martial prominence.

Each feudal ryu committed its history, customs, beliefs, technical

*Two types of stirrup*

characteristics, and actual fighting techniques to writing in the form of *makimono* (hand scrolls). The makimono are the treasures of the ryu, and because they reflect the divine inspiration that brought the ryu into existence, they are religiously revered and carefully safeguarded. Though the historic value of the makimono in any study of Japanese martial culture is great, the contents of these scrolls were never intended to be revealed to those outside the ryu; thus their contents are unavailable to general study. Even were the makimono to be made available, it is unlikely that even Japanese investigators could decipher them. Each ryu used cryptic language, diagrams, and symbols to record its particular matters, and these are unintelligible to all but those who possess sufficient experience as disciples of a ryu.

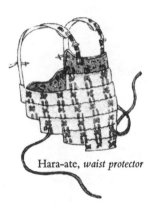

Hara-ate, *waist protector*

Modern-day expert technicians trained in the teachings of the feudal ryu also provide a valuable key to the Japanese martial past. The weight of the moral responsibility upon these men to uphold the teachings of their ryu in an undistorted fashion is extremely heavy; the pressures of modern society work to compel them to compromise their traditions. But when we become familiar with the daily lives of these modern survivors of the classical warrior's culture, we come to understand that the real strength of the classical fighting man was bedded in simple patriotism, rigid discipline, a frugal life, and unwearied cultivation of the bujutsu.

These men demonstrate how the classical warrior trained and fought. Through their dynamic execution of the various components of the bujutsu, as shown in the action photographs in this book, the feudal fighting man lives again and the martial skills of the past are revealed.

We can readily understand that, for the classical warrior, combat was not only a test of stamina and skill but, above all, an ethical matter that was to be entered into only in a prescribed manner. Ill-fitted as he was for wars of territorial expansion because of his inflexible customs, weapons, and fighting arts, the classical warrior was ideally constituted to fight among his own kind. On foreign soil he could expect to face fighting men who, bred on dissimilar ethics, customs, beliefs, and fighting methods, cared nothing for adhering to the Japanese manner of combat. Such an enemy would, as proved by the martial fiascoes on the Asian continent in the past, most likely emerge victorious at the expense of the bushi with his rigid habits. Thus the classical warrior confined himself to combat within his own country.

A valuable secondary source of information about traditional martial culture is *musha-e,* woodblock prints of warriors. From the many thousands of such prints I have selected representative depictions of the classical warrior using his characteristic weapons to supplement the photographs of modern exponents of the bujutsu. It is unimportant to our study whether or not these prints are aesthetically designed or otherwise meet the criteria of the art connoisseur. We need only to be certain that the artists were sufficiently knowledgeable not to make technical errors.

When dealing with the warrior class as a subject, artists composed vivid pictures of the manner in which the warriors trained and fought. So striking are these prints that the warriors of those feudal days seem to come alive and to be showing once again their martial skills and ardor. We receive the impression that for the warrior of classical days, combat was beset with a multitude of situations that tested the man more severely than any other kind of situation. To examine these prints is to watch the warrior as he tightens his bowstring or unsheathes his sword. Indeed, we almost have the impression that we ourselves are the target of his menacing glare and flashing blade. We have no need to strain our imaginations to experience what the event now immortalized in a woodblock print was really like.

When these prints are combined with photographs of classical-warrior types as embodied in present-day practitioners of the martial ryu, the actions of the modern *bugei-sha* (exponents of the bujutsu) are given a heroic cast by those depicted in the woodblock prints, the spirit of which the twentieth-century exponents are trying to preserve. Thus through the mediation of the camera, past and present are brought together and united.

*Hasebe no Nobutsura, a vassal*
*of Yoritomo, under attack*

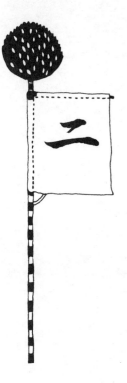

# CHAPTER TWO

# THE CLASSICAL
# WARRIOR
# IN HISTORY

But above all, it is most conducive to the greatness
of empire for a nation to profess the skill of arms
as its principal glory and most honorable employ.

Francis Bacon

The ancient Japanese were hunters and agriculturists before they
were professional warriors; but even so, they always stood ready to
defend themselves when necessary by force of arms. Whether to
fulfill a heavenly mandate, to reap economic rewards, to defend the
reputation or honor of the group, to enhance prestige, or simply for
adventure, Japanese fighting men since prehistoric times have mobi-
lized themselves under specific banners. The dominance of one
local cause over another bred rivals for leadership, and from these
power struggles were produced national ambitions and the necessity
for highly trained warriors to effect their realization.

The warriors known as classical bushi sprang from the shadowy
interplay between military necessity and economic and social factors
produced as the monarchical form of government failed.

As early as the ninth century A.D., a truly professional warrior had
emerged from the warfare and strife that characterized early Japanese
tribal society. He made weapons and fighting arts a condition for the
survival of that society and was eager to earn the prize of wounds.

In the tenth century, the military profession was fully established as a hereditary privilege. Furthermore, each warrior understood combat as his forefathers had understood it: an expectable fact of human life, recurrent in the past and unavoidable in the future. Later, in the twelfth century, because of the lawlessness throughout the land and the corruption that imperiled the decadent court under the domination of the Taira family, Minamoto Yoritomo (1147–99) gathered together certain hardy provincial bushi. He used their redoubtable martial prowess to crush the Taira and bring order to the land. Yoritomo thus made the bushi the undisputed rulers of the nation.

Yoritomo's bakufu was garrisoned at Kamakura, far from the capital city of Kyoto, specifically because he wished to insulate his warriors from the debilitating effects of court society. He had observed how the ease of court life had quickly eroded the martial strength of his enemy predecessors, the Taira, and he wished to avoid the consequences that had befallen them. His bakufu was, in every administrative and executive organ, truly a military government, with its first concern directed toward the discipline and welfare of the bushi who swelled its ranks. But however martially it was oriented, Yoritomo's rule did not overlook justice to others, and under his policies the people of Japan entered upon a short-lived but prosperous era of peace such as they had never known before.

After he had been granted an official sanction by the sovereign to become Japan's first permanent shogun, or generalissimo, Yoritomo became the powerful martial arm of the sovereign and the protector of the imperial court; he was, in fact, the absolute ruler of Japan.

As shogun, Yoritomo decreed that all successors to his office must be of Minamoto stock. He set about building the system by which this process of lineal inheritance could be perpetuated. Inasmuch as

*Two types of military barricade*

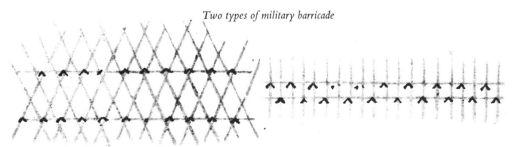

the national characteristics of the Japanese people included a degree of political submission to a personal leader, extreme pride in the solidarity of the group, the acceptance of social and political inequality, a high regard for martial virtues, and the recognition of the obligation of the ruled to be loyal to the ruler, Yoritomo already had a substantial psychological base on which to begin the construction of such a system.

The provincial bushi whom Yoritomo had gathered were an obdurate, illiterate lot, a heterogeneous mixture of fighting men to whom the thought of unifying clans into a centralized unit was completely alien. Furthermore, the concept of loyalty to the sovereign was almost nonexistent; apart from a select few bushi who may have had the privilege of serving as guards at court, the provincial bushi were hardly aware of the sovereign's existence. They were men of aristocratic families in the eastern agricultural regions, where gross lawlessness and, in the northern parts, defense against attacks from the Ainu called for unceasing development of martial arts. Self-reliance had made these men independent of the state. Because the provincial bushi shared common hardships in eking out an

*Scene at the battle of Yamazaki, 1582, between the armies of Toyotomi Hideyoshi and Akechi Mitsuhide*

existence, as well as in battle, they respected the ancient traditions of tribal society, such as the importance of a deep sense of loyalty. No vast gulf existed between these bushi and their immediate superiors because their leaders were also men of high mettle and martial skills.

Among the provincial bushi there were many who were brave, as well as some who were cowardly. There were bushi who took great risks for the sake of glory and honor. When bushi were brave, loyal, or honorable in their actions, they were indeed profoundly so, and the cohesion among such men of moral quality was so great that entire groups, even whole clans, would die in defense of their domains.

Yoritomo admired and demanded fine quality in his bushi. He was aware that the conduct of many bushi of his era was characterized by broken pledges, disobedience to superiors, shifting allegiances that turned the tide of battle, and the placing of material interests before fidelity. And so Yoritomo showed great astuteness in gaining the favor of the provincial bushi. But he never expected to receive a bushi's loyalty on moral grounds alone; he rewarded all bushi well for meritorious services, offering his warriors new writs of investiture or confirming land that they already possessed.

Yoritomo avoided conscripting his fighting men, trusting only professional warriors drawn from the ranks of military families or from those select groups most of whose members stemmed from aristocratic blood. He well knew the difference between the conscript and the professional fighting man; whereas the former was a temporary warrior who was forced to submit to martial discipline, the latter was permanently devoted to his profession and willingly subjected himself to its demands. Professional warriors always fought from disciplined habit; they were obedient instruments and thus were dependable under adverse conditions.

Because Yoritomo demanded bushi with fine qualities, he was conciliatory toward certain of his former foes. He took into his ranks those leading enemy warriors, after their defeat, whom he believed to be sincere in their declarations of loyalty to him. Yoritomo even accepted treacherous acts in his behalf. Iida Goro Ieyoshi

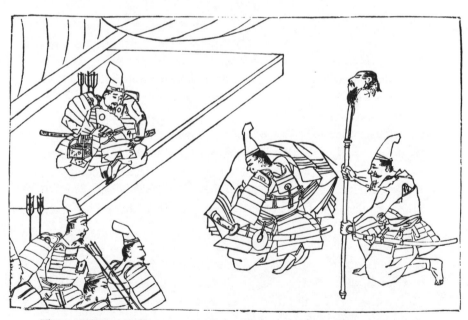

*The warrior Miura Yoshimura presents the head of his brother Taneyoshi to the Kamakura regent, Hojo Yoshitoki, in 1221, thus demonstrating his loyalty to his lord. Taneyoshi had been involved in an anti-bakufu plot and had tried to persuade Yoshimura to join him.*

fought against Yoritomo at the battle of Ishibashiyama but turned against his own commander, who was about to deal Yoritomo a decisive blow; Yoritomo rewarded Ieyoshi and took him into his ranks. But treacherous acts for the sake of reward invoked his wrath. Kiryu Rokuro brought the head of his superior, Fujiwara Toshitsuna, whom Yoritomo was seeking, and asked for a reward. Yoritomo refused the request, denouncing what Rokuro had done as the basest of acts, and beheaded him. So insistent on true loyalty was Yoritomo that when Taira Shigehira was captured and brought before him for sentencing Yoritomo freed Shigehira, after he had requested to be put to death, because the Taira warrior had refused to join Yoritomo and thereby betray his family cause.

Whereas military leaders of the past had generally relied upon bushi of their own clans and excluded all others from their units, Yoritomo valued and welcomed the service of all men of worth without questioning their ancestry. All loyal bushi became his immediate comrades, the equals of the hereditary bushi of his family. He imagined himself to be the leader of all warriors, and thus won the trust of many. Yoritomo had complete military control over almost all bushi, as well as civil authority to appoint or dismiss officials of his bakufu, to confer grants of land and other forms of reward, to confirm the landholdings of warriors, to dispossess them or take other punitive action against them, and to demand such material gifts and services from them as he might deem necessary in connection with the operations of the bakufu. Yoritomo retained the right to post his chosen bushi as public officials on both public and private domains to collect taxes and keep order in the land. He even controlled the selection of the women whom his bushi might marry.

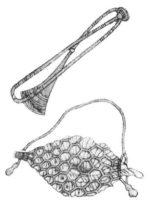

*Bugle and conch horn*

Bushi flocked to Yoritomo's white banner, most of them attracted by the simplicity of his rule. Some were motivated solely by the inspiring martial leadership that Yoritomo provided; others were less idealistic and saw practical advantages in the success of the bakufu, on which their prestige, ranks, rights, and material assets depended. All bushi, however, whether through fear or admiration, considered Yoritomo to be deserving of the title of shogun and absolute ruler.

In general, it can be said that Yoritomo's own actions, in terms of loyalty, exemplified certain principles that he insisted his bushi follow. There could be no split loyalty for warriors in the bakufu. Those dividing their loyalty were severely dealt with, as in the case of Ogino Goro Toshiashige, who was beheaded for deserting his comrades at Ishibashiyama. All bushi were warned to dedicate themselves only to Yoritomo as shogun, and thus loyalty was conceived as being on a direct and personal basis. A bushi's loyalty was officially acknowledged when the shogun confirmed his land-holdings or accepted the man's attendance upon him at Kamakura.

Personal honor was another important ethical consideration in the unwritten code to which all bushi in Yoritomo's bakufu subscribed. The display of honor made loyalty binding in Yoritomo's absolutist system. Breaking the unwritten code was an indelible stain on a bushi's honor and one that only death could mitigate. The bushi might be allowed the privilege of serving his own honor by com-

Seppuku, *ritual self-disembowelment*

mitting *seppuku* (death by self-disembowelment, vulgarly known as *hara-kiri,* "belly-slitting").

Yoritomo expected all bushi to be fully submissive to him. Taira Hirotsune lost his life because he was not. He had been a faithful follower of Yoritomo but was a bit too self-assertive. On one occasion he refused to dismount when meeting Yoritomo; later, when Hirotsune objected to a certain bushi's being given a reward by Yoritomo, he was assassinated by Yoritomo's order. Yoritomo was also extremely critical of the social behavior of his bushi. Sameshima Shiro attacked a fellow bushi during a banquet and had a finger of his right hand cut off as punishment. Bushi who became outlaws were beheaded upon capture, and those who killed such men were amply rewarded.

Gumbai-uchiwa,
*military leader's fans*

Because of the moral bond that existed between himself as shogun and the bushi, Yoritomo could and did execute his men when he doubted their loyalty to him. His younger half-brother and most brilliant field commander, Yoshitsune, was assassinated in 1189 on Yoritomo's order because Yoritomo suspected Yoshitsune of plotting against him. Yoritomo even seduced the daughters and wives of some of his most loyal warriors, it is said, to test the warriors' dedication to him. The bushi whom he offended in this manner could do nothing about it. Any complaint that might be registered brought Yoritomo's instant wrath. The conduct of the shogun was not considered a just reason for a bushi to desert his supreme leader. It remained the ideal of almost every bushi, if he did not look with favor upon the shogun's actions, to commit seppuku rather than go against the will of his august superior. But in practice, as in the case of almost all bushi ideals, this was rarely done.

An outstanding feature of Japanese history is the changes that occurred in martial culture after Yoritomo's death. Some were as obvious as the bakufu's policy of disregarding the need to appoint a competent bushi shogun, others as subtle as shifts in ethical outlook. These changes were both fundamental and fateful.

Though the Hojo family, which took over the direction of the bakufu after Yoritomo's death in 1199, wrought a well-knit form of government and thereby gave to the Japanese nation nearly a century of law and order, the political equilibrium of the country was unstable. This was because the leaders of each component of the duarchy constituting the government were incapable of commanding the respect of the bushi that Yoritomo had. There was the sovereign at Kyoto, whose right to rule was the central doctrine of the national religion, Shinto; there was also a ruler at Kamakura, whose title to govern depended on the strength of the martial power he commanded to discourage any challenge from the court or elsewhere. When that power deteriorated, it was an opportunity not likely to be neglected by the court, ever wishful to regain its lost sway. The fact that the Hojo successors, originally illustrious for the quality of their justice, eventually succumbed to bribes and other corrupt practices was another incentive to action on the part of those who sought the downfall of the oligarchy at Kamakura and the destruction of the Hojo family that led it.

Yoritomo's system of government had been a simple triangular relationship in which Yoritomo, as shogun, occupied the apex. The sides of that triangle, the virtues of honor and loyalty, were subtended by the base of the bujutsu. Thus with Yoritomo gone, and when his successors disrupted the effect of the virtues of honor and loyalty that he had carefully instilled in the bushi code, only the harsh baseline of the triangle, the bujutsu, remained. Sheared of its ethical supports of honor and loyalty, the bujutsu became combatively open-ended and could as easily be used against the bakufu as for it.

The Hojo were able to control Yoritomo's two sons, Yoriie and Sanetomo, who succeeded in turn to the post of shogun, because both proved to be incompetent rulers. Yoriie was exiled and later murdered, in 1204, by the Hojo; Sanetomo was assassinated by a son of Yoriie in 1219. Subsequent shogun, all Hojo-appointed, were not of bushi stock, and although of noble blood, were often mentally and physically weak. These nominal shogun were completely dominated by the Hojo through the post of regent. Some Hojo regents were capable administrators, but all of them lacked the firm hand of the first Minamoto shogun. The last regent, Hojo Takatoki (1303–33), assumed office at the age of thirteen and deputed his responsibilities to an unworthy subordinate while he amused himself with dogfights, drinking bouts, and dancing girls.

*Non-bushi warriors training*

Thus under the ministrations of the Hojo the post of shogun became only the symbol, not the instrument, of authority, and the occupant could be seated and unseated at their whim. Whereas Yoritomo had used a sense of honor to bind together loyalty and martial ardor, his Hojo successors did not. The later Hojo regents' gross neglect of ethical principles invoked the wrath of most bushi. In their attempts to use a system of aesthetics tinged with a modicum of academic education to divert the bushi's martial ardor, the Hojo further alienated them; the strangeness to most bushi of the intellectual landscape guaranteed the failure of this policy.

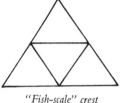

*"Fish-scale" crest of the Hojo clan*

It was a relatively undisciplined environment after Yoritomo, in which the bushi's relations with the shogun were not absolute; nor were they personal or direct. The Hojo greatly feared the loss their influence would sustain if the bushi were linked directly to the shogun, for as regents to the shogun, they were usurpers of power who were supported mainly by their own family members. They could not demand the loyalty of all bushi, as Yoritomo had done, and with the passing of time the Hojo shared the top posts of the bakufu with the members of other leading families with high ambitions. Collective leadership was characteristic of the Hojo bakufu. Bushi were instructed to dedicate their loyalty to the institution—the bakufu—instead of to the shogun personally. Disunity in the conduct of national affairs followed.

The shift in bushi loyalty did little good. Few hardened bushi would draw sword in defense of a nominal leader who could not uphold the stern traditions of the warrior, and even fewer bushi wished to dedicate their loyalty to an organization headed by those who were their inferiors as fighting men. Thus when the Hojo arrested and mistreated Yoriie, Izumi Chikahira, who had been a personal attendant to the shogun, staged a coup d'état, as did Miura Mitsumura when the Hojo deposed his young master, Fujiwara Yoritsune, who had become shogun at the age of eight.

Provincial bushi were spread over a wide territory, and many important warrior families were geographically isolated from one another. Only the most influential of them had any relationship with the shogun. The bakufu, which in Yoritomo's time was paternalistic, became bureaucratic in nature under Hojo domination.

*Ground plan of
a fortress*

This meant, for the majority of bushi, that bakufu intermediaries prevented them from having free access even to the ordinary agencies of the bakufu that they were expected to support.

The falling into abeyance of the custom of primogeniture was especially harmful to continued loyalty to the shogun. Landowners subdivided their holdings without the shogun's consent, and each new landholder thus created became the superior of those in his charge. The large degree of freedom given the bushi in revoking and revising policies, repudiating and disinheriting their children, and dividing their land among family members, whether consanguinary or adopted, also weakened the shogun's hold over them. Furthermore, the practice of subdividing land served to diminish the economic resources of many bushi, and this, apart from making them state liabilities, also made them restless and therefore dangerous sources of disturbance.

Ties with the shogun were still further weakened by the policy of the Hojo bakufu that allowed a bushi to recognize one of the Hojo leaders as his personal superior without at the same time giving up his allegiance to the shogun. Shifting of allegiance also became more common than ever before. The bakufu recognized and sanctioned such shifts, rationalizing the matter by maintaining that no matter whom a bushi chose for his superior, he would ultimately still be under the jurisdiction of the bakufu, which considered itself the constitutional ruler of the whole bushi structure. Only disloyalty that involved the unjust repudiation of a superior, the abandoning of one's superior while retaining land given by him, acts of treachery or rebellion against a superior or against the bakufu, or the disobeying of bakufu laws brought swift governmental retaliation.

It is an incontrovertible fact that the selfish, materialistic desires of some bushi were responsible for the forces that led to the prevalence of the habit of defying a superior. But there were also many instances in which bushi in positions of authority were unjust, and the self-sacrificing loyalty demonstrated by their followers had the effect of disrupting national unity. Though the superior acted in an unethical way, the subject behaved as a loyal subject and did not protest. Dissension among the bushi as well as among the commoners was a characteristic of post-Yoritomo times. This became a

major factor because the Hojo's peaceful rule had insensibly generated a national consciousness, and there was now a wider stream
of public opinion. Bushi harboring personal ambitions became
openly hostile over such matters as rights to the shogunal or regency
succession, the question of political unity for the nation, and whether
or not the sovereign should rule as well as reign.

The evils attendant upon a weak shogun and a still weaker court
became favorable to the establishment of an independent class of
military rulers, each of whom had his own territory. No holder of
territory, however, could feel quite secure in his domains unless he
mustered a large number of warriors who made the constant study
of the bujutsu their profession. With the very legitimacy of the
bakufu in question, it was apparent that, unless a strong bushi leader
were to assume control, this form of government would not endure.

A common danger, in the form of two invasions of Japan by the
Mongols in the late thirteenth century, temporarily submerged the
bushi's growing antagonism toward the bakufu. Bushi valor, together with natural calamity in the form of two typhoons, sent the
Mongol armies reeling back to the Asian continent, thoroughly
beaten and never again to challenge Japan.

During and after the Mongol invasions, the bushi realized that
their belief that the tactic of single combat would always be effective had almost proved disastrous, for the Mongols were specialists
in mass engagement. Only the bushi's fanatic determination to
prevent the Mongols from massing their cavalry had saved the day.
The massive stone wall ten feet high that the bushi had erected along
the shores of Hakata Bay in Kyushu had proved invaluable, as it had
greatly restricted the massing of the Mongol cavalry. Thus methods
of erecting field fortifications, or *chikujo-jutsu,* became one branch
of the bujutsu that was studied anew.

Their direct invasion checked by the stone wall, the Mongols had
attempted to turn the Japanese flanks. Hordes of Chinese warriors,
conscripted by the Mongols for the invasions, met their fate at the
hands of skilled bushi wielding razor-sharp swords. The Chinese,
however, were formidable spearmen. As a result, a new interest
in the spear arose among the bushi. The bushi, on the other hand,
had been highly successful with halberdlike weapons, the *nagamaki*

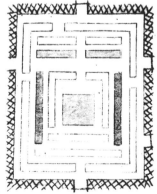

*Plan of an encampment*

*Battling the Mongol invaders*

and *naginata*. As Mongol cavalrymen tried to encircle the wall, they were met by Japanese infantry warriors who chopped off the legs of the Mongol steeds, and as the riders toppled to the ground, they were dealt similar treatment.

Also as a result of the Mongol invasions, armor, which had been in use by Japanese fighting men throughout the ages, was modified to become lighter and more flexible. Swords were shortened and made lighter to permit faster handling.

The bakufu's preparation for defense against possible future invasions by the Mongols continued for almost two decades after the second Mongol invasion had been repelled in 1281. Expenditures necessary to maintain a state of readiness for war had drained the coffers of both the bakufu and the imperial court. It was partly on account of financial embarrassment and partly because the bushi who had fought so valiantly for their country were now highly dissatisfied with their lot that so many opposed the bakufu. Professional warriors expected rewards for their services, because since earliest times such services had always been materially recognized. Even in Yoritomo's time the victorious bushi had been given shares in the spoils. But the operations against the Mongol invasions had been purely defensive, and there were no spoils to divide. Many bushi were also heavily in debt to the growing class of commoners, the merchants and artisans, who had supplied them with the goods and money needed for carrying on the fight.

In addition, many bushi were openly furious that the shogun was not the type of man to command respect; still others detested the bakufu's policy of selecting successors to the throne. The situation headed toward a climax. Finally a treacherous act by a bakufu general, Ashikaga Takauji, who went over to the imperial cause, enabled the imperial forces to overthrow the Hojo-dominated bakufu in 1333. Takauji proved even more treacherous when he seized upon the sovereign's lack of political wisdom to defect from the imperial cause and establish his own sovereign and court, further complicating the issue of imperial legitimacy. This rift continued for more than fifty years. In this way Japan entered the turbulent Ashikaga period (1336–1568).

At this time warriors like Kusunoki Masashige were few. Masashige was the exemplar of the classical bushi, a paragon of martial valor and loyalty, whom neither adversity nor prosperity could alter. He sided with the imperial court at a time when the throne could count on little martial support from the warrior class, depending instead upon the armies of *so-hei,* or warrior-monks, from the great monasteries and on such provincial families as were disenchanted with the Hojo rule or were lessees of court lands and therefore inclined to side with the imperial cause.

The Hojo bakufu quickly recognized Masashige as a dangerous enemy and openly put a price on his head. Any man, however low in social rank, who could prove that he had killed Masashige would receive a substantial tract of land. This was a departure from the traditional policy associated with Yoritomo and the early Hojo bakufu, and one of which they could not even have conceived. Imperial prestige never wavered, as Masashige's courage and martial resource met every challenge. At Chihaya, a fortress on Mount Kongo, he made a gallant defense against the bakufu's determined onslaught, holding off a great army with a handful of men inspired by his brilliant tactics. Chihaya never fell. In his defense of the

*Ashikaga Takauji*

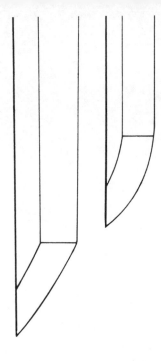

fortress, Masashige demonstrated the quality of his loyalty, without which the imperial cause would surely have been lost.

Though Kusunoki Masashige disliked and distrusted his commander and chief, Nitta Yoshisada, he remained completely loyal to him. At the battle of Minatogawa, when Yoshisada, under heavy attack, withdrew his warriors and thus exposed Masashige to overwhelming odds, the loyalist cause was lost. Masashige died on the field of battle faithfully defending the gross tactical blunder of his superior rather than retreat to safety.

Acts of treachery like those of Ashikaga Takauji lowered the standards of bushi virtues. Bushi loyalty was divided between support for the bakufu on one hand and self-interest on the other. The very ethical values that once had been the mainstays of the classical bushi had fallen into abeyance. Loyalty had always been a moral obligation, but now it took on a contractual aspect as bushi abused the systems of land tenure and taxation; illegal confiscation of land and immunity from taxation were but two of the abuses committed to reap economic rewards. Loyalty derived its sustenance from wealth and was thus transformed into greed. Bushi were quick to forsake ties with their superiors and to make amends with former foes so as to be on the winning side. Martial ardor, exemplified during Yoritomo's time by the bushi's spirit of reckless disregard of personal safety in combat, abated, and many bushi were brave only when bravery was expedient. In addition, there was little willingness to face adversity and no shame in turning on or deserting those comrades on the field of combat who had not preceded them in fast retreat. An utmost concern for staying alive on the field of battle became common, and personal honor became more or less an academic issue. The majority of the bushi of the Ashikaga period were not of the same mettle as the warriors of earlier days. However, even during this age, when close bonds were dissolved or bartered for gain, some bushi steadfastly adhered to the traditional values. Their names are deeply impressed on the pages of history.

An old society was disappearing, and in its stead a new form of social cohesion began to appear. But the vast diffusion of martial power that accompanied it gave opportunities and responsibilities to non-bushi in charting the course of the reunification of the nation.

There followed an infamous period, the *sengoku jidai,* or age of the country at war, when violence became the order of the day. From the standpoint of bujutsu it was a technically productive era, although from an ethical standpoint it showed a sharp decline in the standards of the bushi. Japanese martial culture was undergoing radical changes.

Ashikaga Takauji's initial popularity with the bushi was overwhelmingly high, perhaps because he was himself a bushi and a successful field general. He gained support from the bushi and founded a bakufu, which he garrisoned at Kyoto, receiving sanction from his sovereign to become shogun. The Ashikaga bakufu did not recognize classical virtues any more than Takauji did. His bakufu soon encroached upon all imperial prerogatives, ushering in a period of high living and general moral decline modified by certain advances in intellectual and aesthetic disciplines. Takauji's successors as shogun were even less admirable than he.

The post of shogun became, in the words of a courtier, "as trifling as a bird flitting in a tree." The power of the bakufu soon diminished until it had only nominal control of the central provinces. Bakufu justice became extremely corrupt, and the courts were full of undecided suits. The people of the nation were in an uproar, and, as bushi deserted their bakufu posts, there was no way to check the chaos that had descended on Japan. Political power passed into the hands of lower-ranking bushi and civilians. Subordinates drove out their superiors and took over as rulers of provinces; farmers and townspeople were so miserable that they rioted en masse, protesting their interests by armed force. This was an age in which every man acted according to his own best interests. Even the courtiers and the shogun became poverty-stricken, and any remaining dignity was lost.

These chaotic conditions initiated some of the most revolutionary changes ever in Japanese culture. One significant feature of the period was the rise of the daimyo, or great names: powerful landowners, some of whom were bushi, who had risen by various means—usually corrupt or devious—from aristocratic or lower social levels to become the virtual rulers of independent domains. It was these daimyo who influenced the growth of a variety of

*Sword blades*

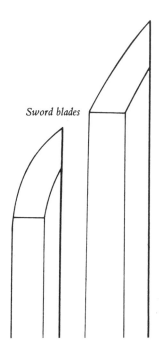

aspects of Japanese feudalistic culture, including the martial ryu.

In order that a daimyo might control his domain and preserve it from the encroachment of some other ambitious daimyo, who would most certainly resort to armed force, it was necessary for him to muster a standing body of fighting men. Bushi made up only a part of this body. A new class of fighting men appeared, known as *nobushi,* or field warriors, or as *ashigaru,* which means "light-footed soldiers." These men came from those field workers who were high-spirited enough to enjoy becoming pawns in the national chaos; they had no way to become bushi. At times reliable soldiers, they were more often just provincial rowdies, robbers, or mercenaries who had chosen a life of adventure and who offered their professional services and a thin veneer of loyalty to anyone who would guarantee them a livelihood.

The daimyo also realized that the productivity of their domains could not be maintained if they caused their labor force to revolt because of oppressive practices, so they adopted the policy of protecting the labor force from ill treatment. Moreover, they thus added to the prestige of the commoners. Since in times of martial emergency every man was a fighting man, the daimyo began to conscript farmers and other peasants to serve alongside the bushi and nobushi. The hardy farmers proved to be excellent fighters after exposure to a minimum of martial discipline; farmers grew accustomed to hastening from their fields to the battleground. In their new and important role they became known as *ji-samurai,* or farmer-warriors.

Thus commoners, as nobushi and ji-samurai, broke the virtual bushi monopoly of the profession of arms. From the ranks of these commoners came the effective strength for future insurrections whenever the common men's grievances were not heard or heeded. In time their collective strength was to cause great anxiety to the leaders of Japan.

Classical bushi were now in a minority when the daimyo mustered their martial forces. They were also unhappy over the fact that commoners had ready access to some of the martial ryu. But the bushi stood adamant in the face of the loss of their monopoly of the martial profession and the narrowing gap dividing them from

*Warrior with bow*

commoners. One socially distinctive badge that still distinguished the bushi from the commoner fighting man was the right to wear two swords; the nobushi and ji-samurai were permitted to wear only one short sword.

With the passing of time the nobushi and ji-samurai became increasingly necessary in the armies of those endeavoring to unify the country. But it took both special men and means to make the commoners formidable in battle. The means preceded the men, because Portuguese arrived from Europe in the mid-sixteenth century, bringing with them the first firearms that the Japanese had ever seen.

Takeda Shingen, born in 1521 to an influential warrior family of Kai Province, tasted his first victory at the age of twenty fighting the oppressive warrior landowners in the rugged wilderness of Shinano Province. Shingen matured into a remarkably able tactician and resolute warrior who, thought he made enemies of the powerful Oda, Imagawa, Hojo, and Uesugi family warriors at one time, fought thirty-eight battles and was never defeated by any of them. Shingen specialized in attack. Four battle banners inscribed with mottoes were carried by his men, one at the head of each of his units. They read: "Quick as wind," "Still as a forest," "Conquer like fire," and "Immovable as a mountain." Each unit was trained to live up to its particular motto.

Shingen believed that any battle could be won if the commander would but implement a carefully thought out strategy. When asked by his officers why he built no castle to serve as a headquarters, Shingen replied: "A warrior-leader must build a castle in the heart of every one of his bushi, and this will be stronger than any material one." This remark demonstrates the importance he placed on the classical bushi virtues of loyalty and honor. He demanded absolute adherence to classical bushi ethics by all his fighting men and recorded this code with precision in his *Kai no Gunritsu* (The Military Discipline of Kai). For all his dependence upon classical martial tradition, however, Shingen was not reluctant to make technical modifications should they produce practical results of value. He made good use of commoners in his ranks, recruiting such farmers and nobushi as would fit into his rigid pattern of martial discipline.

*Armor mask*

Shingen also recognized the importance of firearms and founded a ryu based on their use.

Uesugi Kenshin, the daimyo of Echigo, on the west coast of Japan, conducted numerous campaigns against Shingen. Kenshin was a far less clever tactician than Shingen and therefore found it even more necessary to rely on firearms. He offered rewards to peasants if they would join his forces and succeeded in collecting a heterogeneous following of men who wore shabby armor and

*Musket*

*Marksman with musket*

carried whatever weapons as they could find. In spite of its short-comings Kenshin's peasant army wreaked havoc with Shingen's classical-bushi units, but Kenshin's campaigns won him no particular gains.

If bushi like Takeda Shingen and Uesugi Kenshin can be accused of developing hybrid martial systems in which the classical martial traditions were preserved only to an incomplete degree, then Oda Nobunaga (1534–82) can be named the destroyer of the classical bushi tradition. Through his rapid rise as a statesman-warrior, he effected some of the most significant changes in Japanese martial culture.

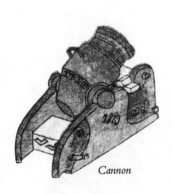

*Cannon*

Nobunaga stemmed from an old family that had provided men to serve with the Ashikaga. He had inherited his father's province of Owari and served there as the highly successful leader of a band of nobushi. The prestige and power of the Ashikaga government had fallen almost to nil, and Nobunaga's martial abilities caught the attention of the sovereign, who strongly urged him to undertake the pacification and unification of the country. Nobunaga's strategy produced decisive results. After consolidating his immediate position in Owari, he occupied Kyoto; a short while later, when the shogun plotted against him, Nobunaga deposed him and brought the Ashikaga regime to an end. Nobunaga ruled with an iron fist; but intense conflicts, centered essentially on the daimyo and their autonomous domains, led to a period in which loyalty and honor had even less value than before. His own general, Akechi Mitsuhide, took Nobunaga's life.

Though he had never formally studied martial disciplines, Nobunaga had the ability to devise applications that proved beyond all doubt that bushi who adhered to the classical bujutsu were less effective in actual combat than commoners armed with firearms. At Nagashino, in 1575, Nobunaga's nobushi and conscript army,

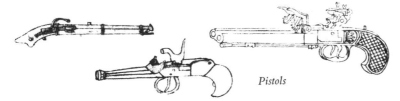

*Pistols*

using firearms, slew wave after wave of classical bushi under the command of Takeda Katsuyori.

Effective as firearms were known to be, they caused heated controversy among the bushi. The classical bushi argued that even a coward armed with a musket could defeat the most courageous and skillful swordsman. To shoot and kill the enemy from afar was one thing, to close with him and cross blades an entirely different matter. Combat, to the classical bushi, was an exercise in moral courage manifested in physical skill. Accordingly, all defenders of the old martial tradition considered the use of firearms to be the tactics of cowards and far beneath the dignity of a true warrior. Many of them refused to use guns.

There was yet another consideration advanced by the classical bushi. The use of firearms deprived a man of a chance to learn how to fight hand to hand. Reliance upon the *corpus vile*—the musket— would lead to the loss of traditional fighting skills. Some bushi were content to have firearms used by the nobushi and ji-samurai, themselves depending only on their traditional weapons. Many such bushi became military commanders of nobushi and conscript fighting men in the service of daimyo.

In spite of heated protests over the use of firearms, the adoption of these weapons as a component of the bujutsu was assured after Nobunaga's victory at Nagashino. It was a clear-cut matter of

*Cannon*

expediency. The new martial art was known as *hojutsu*, or fire art.

The typical fighting man of the late sixteenth century was less interested in how victory was achieved than in the fact that the victory was in his favor. Firearms, especially when used against warriors fighting in the traditional manner, were powerful weapons, to be respected, and provided an advantage that no commander of troops could ignore. Another practical point was that the training of a classical bushi could be completed only after countless hours of exhausting martial discipline, usually totaling more than three years. The time needed for this training, when there were wars to be fought and quickly won (for such was the tempo of the times) was prohibitive. Delays in massing trained fighters were costly in terms of indecisive combat. A commoner could be trained to be an effective fighting man, if armed with a musket, in less than half a year.

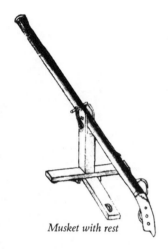

*Musket with rest*

The conduct of war underwent modifications to accommodate the use of firearms. *Senjo-jutsu*, a component of the bujutsu dealing with tactics, and *chikujo-jutsu*, the art of field fortifications, were revised for similar reasons. Defensive armor became somewhat more protective in design, in attempts to prevent bullets and ball from piercing it.

Toyotomi Hideyoshi (1536–98) was not in the least reluctant to follow the lead of Nobunaga, his former commander, on the stage of national affairs. After avenging Nobunaga's assassination at the battle of Yamazaki, and because he stood at the head of a powerful and victorious martial force, Hideyoshi moved with precision and seized the political initiative; by the late sixteenth century he had succeeded in unifying the country. This remarkable man, although not of bushi stock, is recognized as one of Japan's greatest generals. Whereas Nobunaga had encouraged the rise of commoners to positions of authority in his government, Hideyoshi was firmly against such a liberal policy. As a consequence, he set the basis for militarism in Japan.

Daimyo who continued to instigate intrigues to gain economic or political advantage jeopardized the chances for national stability. To forestall such attempts Hideyoshi struck at the daimyo's source of martial strength—the nobushi mercenaries and conscript ji-samurai, who had gradually replaced the daimyo armies of bushi.

*Toyotomi Hideyoshi*

He issued an edict that in effect forbade a commoner to have any weapon in his possession. Those commoners who had already become nobushi or ji-samurai, and who were actually serving daimyo, were exempted from the provisions of this edict; furthermore, they were to be considered bushi. Another edict forbade social mobility; no peasant could abandon his work to take up a trade or become a laborer, no bushi could leave his immediate superior without permission, and no bushi could give up his profession to become a laborer or farmer.

Hideyoshi's policies had the effect of drawing a marked distinction between fighting men and commoners. To some extent these policies also caused the source of hereditary fighting men to dwindle still more by discouraging the solidarity of rural families. And from Hideyoshi's time on, posts in the bushi complex, which had absorbed a great number of commoners, thus came to be filled by men who

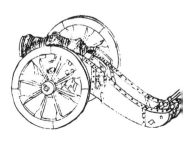

*Cannon*

had not the slightest professional interest in classical martial traditions or methods.

After Hideyoshi's death Tokugawa Ieyasu (1542–1616), a general who had been selected by Hideyoshi to carry on the work of unifying the nation, gained the upper hand by winning an engagement over those who sought to wrest the reins of government from him. At Sekigahara, in 1600, Ieyasu directed a stunning military victory over his foes. He then established the Tokugawa bakufu at Edo (now Tokyo) and became its first shogun. His two immediate successors maintained the bakufu in the military style its founder had intended, but thereafter it was reduced to anything but a military government. Despite the feeble attempts of a few shogun, the bakufu came under the almost total control of civilian officials whose policy it was to paralyze the commoners' initiative by educating them to be content with the status quo. Their administration, tinged with Neo-Confucian philosophy, gave the nation 265 years of relative peace and stability and insulated it from international affairs through a strict policy of isolationism. Nevertheless, from the time of the fourth shogun a growing anti-bakufu sentiment became evident.

The collapse of the bakufu in the mid-nineteenth century was caused by a combination of factors, an important one being the disunity between bushi and civilians over the matter of monarchical rule and the problem of how to deal with intruding Westerners. With the fall of the bakufu many feudal institutions became obsolete, including the martial ryu and the bujutsu. But survival is innate in the bujutsu, itself the study of self-defense, and thus the classical martial arts and their ryu survived the onslaughts of time.

*Hollyhock crest of the Tokugawa*

It is not necessary for us to study Japanese history after the collapse of the Tokugawa bakufu. There is plenty of evidence to show that the Tokugawa period was characterized by lack of support for the classical bushi and their traditions, as well as to show the general decline of the quasi-bushi system that had replaced them. A summary of some of the essential features of Tokugawa martial culture will clearly reveal the great contrast in ideals and mechanisms separating it from classical bushi traditions. In the flow of great conflict between unification and disunity, receptivity and seclusion, that characterizes Tokugawa history, it is not hard to understand

*Tokugawa Ieyasu*

that the classical martial traditions, which in Tokugawa times were ineffective as a ruling force, had been replaced by elements that proved to be the seeds of modern militarism.

Hideyoshi's move to build up a military class was not a new idea. However, through his edicts forbidding social mobility and the bearing of arms by commoners, Hideyoshi brought about something that had not been accomplished even in Yoritomo's time: the creation of an absolute military caste system. There had always been some degree of social mobility, however difficult it had been to achieve, and there had never been strict enforcement of any ban on the possession or carrying of weapons.

The establishment of an absolute caste system is an essential feature of militarism, and the Tokugawa government built up a fully militaristic society first by accepting Hideyoshi's edicts and then by making them even more rigid through later legislation. The

*Various kinds of shot*

government exhibited other features of militarism that the earlier bakufu had lacked. It amassed large numbers of bushi and quantities of materiel solely for the perpetuation of customs, interests, and actions that were supposedly associated with martial disciplines but that actually transcended martial purpose. The Tokugawa built its armies to ensure the perpetual influence of its own family, not to wage war. In so doing, it discouraged martial imagination and inventiveness, a policy that in the long run eroded martial skill.

In the pursuance of its policies the Tokugawa government lost its social and political equilibrium. In its overemphasis on the preservation of social class, cult, and hereditary authority, and in its belief in and false social foundations for a privileged stratum of so-called fighting men, the shogunate engendered a narcissistic military spirit that through its neglect of martial reality led to a waste of manpower in unproductive service.

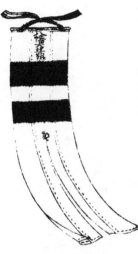

Tenaga-hata *banner*

The bushi of the Tokugawa bakufu, with rare exceptions, can be characterized as upstarts, who, unable to trace their ancestry legitimately into prestigious lines, falsified genealogical records to obtain the necessary prestige for entry into high posts in the bakufu. These vain men enjoyed every advantage over other commoners, conveniently forgetting the social level from which they had come. They oppressed their former social equals through their newly and falsely acquired social seniority. They also hid behind other artificial social and legal barriers, such as false honors, a pompous manner, the exercise of undue power, and basking in an undeserved martial glory reflected by a past with which they had no relationship. Even the best of them were bushi only by birthright, not through long active service as fighting men, which was the criterion of the classical warrior. The *hatamoto,* or banner men, the top rank of bushi, were particularly reprehensible social misfits who increased the feeling of general dislike the public held for Tokugawa-bakufu bushi; the few genuine classical bushi who remained also had nothing but contempt for the Tokugawa bakufu, because it was filled with morally hollow and emotionally unstable men who had come to fear war and who in times of peace proclaimed parrotlike the virtues of the classical bushi, implying that these virtues were their own.

There is ample evidence that the bakufu became an ethical and legal straitjacket for the bushi class in general. The bakufu kept all bushi overly busy and financially overstrained. The pomp and ceremony that supported such a governmental attitude led those closest to the government to act in an overbearing manner. It was inevitable that the quality of the Tokugawa bushi would decline. Added to the long period of peace that the nation enjoyed was the fact that most Tokugawa bushi had become indolent. In the face of their lack of skill in such martial attainments as riding, shooting, swimming, and use of the sword and other weapons, one greatly angered shogun found it expedient to call in provincial bushi to act as their instructors in bujutsu. This gross humiliation did little more than stimulate a temporary interest in the martial arts.

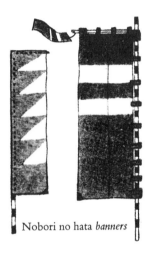

Nobori no hata *banners*

The Tokugawa bushi became known for their lukewarm valor when any of them was given an opportunity to fight. The provincial bushi, on the contrary, remained firm in their fighting spirit because they lived in a severe environment. There, in the rugged countryside, the vestiges of the classical martial ryu continued to inspire fighting men in the fervent belief that the virtues of loyalty and honor were indispensable characteristics of the true warrior. The value and power of their convictions would, in time, smolder and become anti-bakufu, and would eventually determine the downfall of the Tokugawa regime.

The general decline of the Tokugawa bushi's martial skills may be clearly seen in the modifications of the *mitsu-dogu,* the three classical weapons used in concert for restraining swordsmen. These weapons are the *sasumata,* a forked device; the *sodegarami,* a barbed device; and the *tsukubo,* a T-shaped device. All three weapons were provided with very long shafts to protect their users from a skillful swordsman's blade. In the Tokugawa period, these weapons became mere ornamental objects, few bushi knowing how to use them in combat. They were replaced by three other weapons, used largely against bushi by Tokugawa policemen: the *jutte,* a forked iron truncheon; the *manriki-gusari,* a length of weighted chain; and the *rokushaku-bo,* a six-foot hardwood staff. With the exception of the last, these weapons were quite short in length, a feature that required those using them to come very close to the person being apprehended. Generally speaking, the three new weapons were employed independently of one another. Rather than this being a testimony to the skill of those using them, it is indicative of lack of skill in the swordsmen being apprehended. The new restraining weapons, with the possible exception of the staff, would not have proved effective against classical swordsmen.

In the Tokugawa period, as peace settled over the nation, armor gathered dust and systems of unarmed combat began to flourish. Proficiency at *jujutsu,* a generic term coined in Tokugawa times for a variety of systems used in fighting, its exponents being minimally armed, became the measure of fighting ability. In many systems of jujutsu no weapons were used. Their techniques were based on abstract ideas derived from Chinese philosophy, and the axiom *ju yoku go o sei suru,* "flexibility masters hardness," became their central theme. The Japanese broadened the meaning of this axiom, giving it such connotations as "the soft conquers the hard," "the weak turns aside the strong," and "in yielding there is strength." There had always been a certain amount of "flexibility" and "yielding" present in the fighting techniques of the classical warriors, but never had there been complete reliance upon such factors in combat. The emphasis placed on such intellectual considerations led directly to a loss in effectiveness of the systems that were entirely based on these factors. The classical warriors' intention that fighting arts should be effective in combat was replaced by the satisfaction derived from their rhythmic form, and aesthetic pleasure became the object of many systems of jujutsu.

The stern martial spirit of the past was thus weakened during Tokugawa times with the passing of martial endeavor from a combative sphere to one in which the individual's pleasure was paramount. It was an age in which the desire for self-protection gave way to one of self-perfection, characterized by the loss of importance of the martial arts (bujutsu) and the development and growing prestige of the martial ways (budo).

Whatever residual value the methods of the classical bushi might have had for the Tokugawa bushi was summarily nullified by the bakufu's military attacks against what were termed *choteki,* or rebels, at Sekigahara (1600), Osaka Castle (1614–15), and Shimabara (1638). At these places hundreds of thousands of classical bushi died, wiped

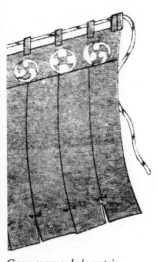

*Camp commander's curtain*

out by bakufu firepower. Thereafter, the classical bushi, no longer
an effective social force, dwindled to a small number of people
living in isolated groups. The classical bushi would rise again when
government policies angered them and heated their blades, but the
outcome would not be in their favor. The fact that firearms had to
be resorted to in quelling the classical bushi is perhaps the finest
compliment to their worth as fighting men that can be paid them.
There was obviously no group of fighting men in Japan who could
defeat them by any other means.

*Nasu no Yoichi*

# CHAPTER THREE

# DEVELOPMENT OF THE BUJUTSU

What a perversion of morality to wish to abolish
heroism among men.

Heinrich von Treitschke

The need for more effective means of combat had stimulated even
the earliest Japanese fighting men to make widespread study of
weapons and their uses, but there was little standardization of
weapons or systematization of fighting arts until after the emergence
of the professional warrior class. Bushi who had come out of the
terrible combats alive and had thereby earned a high degree of
respect from others, since renown is easily won on the battlefield,
conducted most of the investigations. From about the late twelfth
century onward, the results of such findings were systematized, then
consolidated through the founding of martial ryu. The major
weapons—bow and arrow, sword, spear, and halberd—received the
major emphasis, but no weapon or fighting method that could be
proved to be effective was overlooked. By the seventeenth century
some sixty different fighting systems in almost nine thousand formal
traditions, or ryu, had been developed, thus making the bujutsu a
formidable corpus.

Significantly, the importance of the martial ryu was recognized
from the time of the Kamakura bakufu, and the bakufu eagerly
sought out the best headmasters and technicians as instructors. Those
ryu that did not desire to cooperate with or were not selected by
the bakufu developed as martial traditions in private domains.

Whereas it is true that by modern standards the classical martial ryu dealt in unalterable customs, weapons, and fighting arts, the persistence of this attitude down to the twentieth century is indicative of the unswerving dedication of their members, not the inability of these warriors to invent, accept, adapt, or adopt new ideas.

Each ryu developed particular technical features that made it unique. These beliefs and practices were considered the heritage of the ryu and were forbidden to outsiders. As time passed, compartmentalization of the numerous ryu became unavoidable, and bitter professional jealousies came to the surface. With consequent displays of passion to prove which tradition was superior to all others, combat between technicians of the different ryu became commonplace. The desire to find more effective ways to dispatch a foe provided a splendid opportunity for a still wider proliferation of the bujutsu.

The bujutsu, being realistic fighting skills, include both military and naval aspects. Though primarily concerned with the methods of using different types of weapons, especially the sword, spear, and halberd, they also include auxiliary systems that act as adjuncts to enhance the employment of weapons: the arts of building field fortifications, making signal fires, and even contriving strategy and tactics are but a few such skills that fall within the province of the bujutsu.

Because the bujutsu stood as the symbol and instrument of bushi strength and vitality, their study was declared the exclusive prerogative of the professional warrior class. Commoners, while not totally without weapons, nevertheless were forbidden to possess the types used by the bushi and were refused permission to study the bujutsu.

*Signal fire*

Two facts had been clear to Yoritomo from his knowledge of the past. The first was that armed force, though not the only means by which his nation could be governed, could never be wholly banished from the affairs of state. The second was the fact that loyalty grew best when there was pride in martial skill; for martial skill reflects pride in oneself and evokes a sense of honor to maintain that pride. Yoritomo had gained the bushi's loyalty because he was himself a bushi who could shoot a bow or wield a sword along with the best of them. He was also in full agreement with the bushi that every warrior should always be ready to fight efficiently when necessary; most bushi thought all else was merely self-aggrandizement. Yoritomo demanded of his warriors constant study and practice of the bujutsu.

A classical bushi was thus honor bound to be an efficient fighting man loyal to the shogun. Serious breaches of the loyalty expected

*Portion of a scroll containing teachings of a martial* ryu

would most likely bring the wrath of the bakufu to bear upon himself, as well as on the local group in which he functioned. The bushi trusted implicitly in bujutsu to arouse in him a proper attitude, one worthy of trust and respect from others. He thought it spiritless to gain by sweat alone that which could be won by a combination of sweat and danger; this way of thinking led to the bushi's disdain for those of the lower social strata, who through their sweat earned the means to live.

Arduous daily training in the martial disciplines became the earmark of all bushi. Such untiring efforts included a very thorough grounding in *omote,* or surface techniques, usually a three- or four-year process, which extended to the most minute details. Through the practice of omote the bushi familiarized himself with the basic handling of his arms as rigidly prescribed by the martial tradition to which he subscribed. From this basic foundation he entered higher skills, the *okuden,* or secret teachings, which brought finesse to his fighting ability. His success in combat depended upon mastery of this, the highest category of techniques.

These innermost secrets of the martial ryu gave him much confi-

*Portion of a* ryu *scroll showing* kenjutsu *techniques*

dence, for he knew that when he faced the ultimate test—combat—he would be equipped with lightning-quick reflexes. Furthermore, the multitude of technical details impressed upon the bushi by the okuden taught him the capabilities and limitations of each and every combative action. He knew, for instance, that thrusting his sword into an enemy's midsection, even to the depth of only a fraction of an inch, would unerringly prevent the enemy from completing an overhead-downward stroke of his weapon, and that there was thus absolutely no danger in being directly under the enemy's weapon. In contrast, he also knew that if he slashed the undersurface of the enemy's wrist hard enough almost to sever the hand, the enemy could and would continue an overhead-downward stroke.

But the bujutsu was still more to the classical bushi. It was an educative process by which certain virtues were exalted as martial mores: courage, self-reliance, self-sacrifice, obedience, discipline, patience, careful judgment, courtesy, and frugality were learned concomitant with the development of technical skills. Any tendency of the individual bushi to deviate from what was expected of him was eliminated through the threat of disciplinary action—including death—by the ryu. Accordingly, the classical bushi grew to be an elite group of fighting men with the very highest esprit de corps.

It was not by chance or coincidence that the bujutsu were developed and maintained. These fighting arts took on systematic form because the bushi limited and directed their study by means of a steering device called *kata,* or prearranged form. Kata became, and remains today, the central training method for all bujutsu. It is the only way by which the action that characterizes the bujutsu can be practiced without the practitioner's being wounded or killed.

Largely for economic reasons, but also in order to have a margin of safety, exponents of the bujutsu traditionally employed a training weapon made of a special kind of hardwood. Metal weapons were also used, but if used in daily training they would soon become broken or otherwise damaged, whereas the wooden substitutes proved more durable and far less costly to replace. The relative safety afforded by the wooden weapons was another obvious advantage.

*Two types of quiver*

Wooden weapons, however, must not be seen as inferior substitutes for metal ones. In many types of combat they are superior to their metal counterparts. The most famous of all Japanese swordsmen, Miyamoto Musashi (1584?–1645), preferred the *bokken,* or wooden sword, in combat simply because it was indestructible.

Prior to the Kamakura period, warriors generally rode horseback. Astride fast horses, a rowdy lot and relatively undisciplined, they rode fearlessly into battle, where they depended on single combat

*The great seventeenth-century swordsman Miyamoto Musashi training with two* bokken, *or wooden swords. He made this method of* kenjutsu *famous, and his preference for two blades gave him a dexterity unrivaled by any other swordsman of his day.*      ▷

to decide issues. They wore armor and were armed with bow and arrows, the former being a magnificently constructed, asymmetrical longbow with a powerful range. They also carried a razor-sharp long sword, called a *tachi,* which hung from a special slinglike harness worn on the left hip. This long sword was carried with its single, convex cutting edge downward. This custom necessitated a "ground to sky" draw, an advantage when used from horseback. Under Yoritomo new and improved weapons were developed, and bushi tended to specialize in certain types; as a result tactics became more sophisticated. Missile weapons, while not entirely outmoded, were to some extent displaced by those that pierce or strike: the *yari,* or spear; the *nagamaki* and *naginata,* both halberds; and the *bo,* or staff. Even the sword was modified.

Though warriors on horseback enjoyed aristocratic prestige (for only the wealthy could afford armor, suitable mounts, and keen, durable swords), what had been proven in earlier eras was quickly reconfirmed, that infantry-based tactics had considerable value in bringing a combat to an end. The use of the long cavalry sword, with its "ground to sky" draw, however, proved less efficient when used from the ground than a sword that was slightly shorter and worn thrust through the warrior's sash, cutting edge upward. This weapon, called a *katana,* was, like the tachi, a curved, single-edged blade. It could be drawn swiftly and accurately with a "sky to ground" action that could easily sever an enemy's arm or leg, or shorten him by the length of his head, at a single stroke. An even shorter sword, the *wakizashi,* was similar to the katana in design but was intended to be used solely with one hand. It was worn thrust through the sash, in a position just inside that of the katana, where it served as an auxiliary blade. These two swords—the katana and the wakizashi—were known as *daisho,* or large and small. The privilege of wearing the daisho became the distinctive badge of the warrior.

Armor, which had been worn to deflect arrows in flight and the thrusts or slashes of other weapons, served the same purpose for the foot warrior that it did for the mounted one. But it had to be modified to make it lighter and more flexible so that the foot warrior could be agile in combat.

*Warriors in armor*

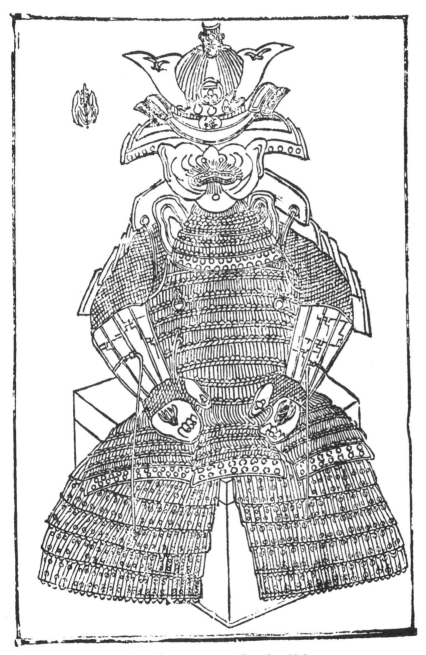

*Sixteenth–century armor with mask and helmet*

*Scene at the battle of Yamazaki, 1582*

*Taira no Tadamori,
twelfth-century
warrior*

The outcome of any combat depended absolutely on timing and insight. Most were preceded by strict, formal procedures designed to put the combatants about to engage each other into the proper frame of mind. A classical warrior, after selecting his adversary, would intone a recitation, sometimes quite lengthy, mainly to intimidate his foe: "I am Sato Shigenobu, second son of Masayuki, the most skillful and feared *kenshi* [expert swordsman] of the Chujo Ryu. I have been in sixteen combats and have never suffered a wound. I mean to make you feel the sharp sting of my magnificent blade, the Sune-kiri [Shin-cutter], a treasured heirloom of my family. With this blade my ancestors slew great numbers of the enemy. Now—prepare to die!"

Since the field of combat was a place of honor, after delivering his recitation the warrior would permit his foe to do likewise: "You have had the misfortune to face me, Yukimitsu Tadao, the descendant of the best swordsman in all Japan. I am the fearless bushi who alone is responsible for the deaths of more than thirty of your ryu's best experts. Your clumsy style has no chance against me. This is your last combat, for I shall dispatch you with my specialty, the *gyaku kesa-age* [a reverse-diagonal stroke]. Advance to your doom!"

Once the combat began it was indeed a *shinken shobu*, a fight to the finish. The victor was privileged to take the head of the vanquished as a symbol of his victory, but this was mainly as a kind of receipt, for the head, when brought before the victor's commander, would afford proof of skill; the bushi could expect a reward, especially if he had slain some famous warrior.

Combat between two individuals—single combat—was characteristic of the early periods of Japanese history and was principally of two types, that conducted at long range and that at close quarters. There was a great difference in engaging the enemy from afar with a projectile weapon, such as the bow and arrow, and in closing with him for close-quarter action, as was necessitated when using the sword or other weapons of the pierce-and-strike variety. Thus the bushi of classical times was forced to develop self-discipline, largely to control fear. "Fear is distributed," notes an old bushi adage, in reference to the *ma-ai,* or combative-engagement distance.

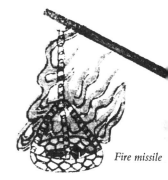

*Fire missile*

*Heads displayed following a battle*

Ma-ai is the distance at which combatants engage each other; as this distance is shortened, the courage and skill of the warrior must be increased.

The bushi also depended on *zanshin,* literally "alertness remaining-form": this term signifies physical form united with mental acuity and concentration, resulting in uninterrupted dominance over the adversary. There could be no effective fighting skill without it. Zanshin was the undeniable mark of the expert technician; it could not be faked. It was the result of countless hours of experience in combative training and was expressed through physical posture. Through zanshin the bushi achieved the proper mental and physical attitude with which to dominate his adversary.

The precise ma-ai used for each combative situation varied according to the weapon being used and that being faced. For each particular circumstance the bushi was expected to know how to position himself so as to create an advantage for himself and a dis-advantage for his enemy. Because of this important consideration, martial ryu were compelled to strive for balance within their curricula. Each ryu, if it hoped to survive the test of combat, re-quired the study and practice of a wide range of weapons. A bushi so trained would seldom face a weapon of whose capabilities and limitations he was entirely ignorant. Thus, in addition to his primary weapon, the *odachi,* or long sword, each bushi achieved some degree of expertise with weapons like the short sword, the spear, the halberd, the throwing knife, and the stick or staff.

In order to understand the nature of these weapons, their com-bative uses, and how the bushi trained to use them, in the following six chapters we will take a detailed look at each major component of the classical bujutsu.

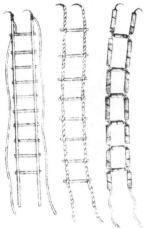

*Scaling ladders*

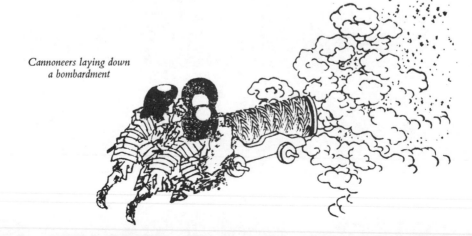

*Cannoneers laying down
a bombardment*

Part Two

# THE WEAPONS
# AND THEIR USE

# CHAPTER FOUR

# BLADED WEAPONS

They bleed on both sides.
Shakespeare

KENJUTSU   It was inevitable that the classical bushi, who lived by the sword, would show the greatest reverence for this, the chief emblem and instrument of their martial power. Japanese mythology and Shinto rites, including that of the sovereign's enthronement ceremony, stand as emphatic witness to the fact that the sword was the premier weapon of the land, serving both a ceremonial and a martial purpose.

Japanese knowledge of metal swordmaking antedates the Christian era by at least two centuries. The greatest swords were personified and even deified, a custom that persists today. They were named just as carefully as were the men who wielded them. Many swords were proclaimed *kami* (extraordinary beings), an indication of the divine attributes and supreme qualities that they were believed to possess. Japanese literature relates tales about magnificent swords that were kami and that gave birth to other kami, of swords that came and went of themselves and that even ventured across the seas, of swords that magically left their scabbards to fight for their possessors in times of danger, of swords that punished profanation with disease and death, and of swords that healed sickness and responded to prayer. The very succession of a claimant to the imperial throne, to this day, cannot be legitimatized without the possession of the *Sanshu no Shinki,* the Three Sacred Regalia, which include the very greatest of Japanese swords, the Kusanagi no Tsurugi of the imperial family.

The development of a functional iron sword of a distinctly

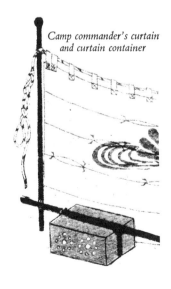

*Camp commander's curtain and curtain container*

*The sixteenth-century warrior Katō Kiyomasa (background) watches a combat between Kimura Matazo (left) and Inoue Daikuro. Matazo threatens Daikuro's face with his blade, while the latter prepares either to parry Matazo's sword or to slash at his right wrist.*

Odachi, kodachi, *and* tanto

Japanese style, the *Nihon-to,* became mandatory with the rise of the professional warrior. Amakuni (c. A.D. 700) is traditionally considered to be the first Japanese swordsmith to produce this type of sword, which featured a curved, single-edged blade. This became the standard sword preferred by all warriors.

Once in possession of a standard sword, the classical warrior understandably made it his central weapon and devised methods by which it could be most effectively used. These methods, called *kenjutsu,* or sword art, became the highest testimony to the bushi's martial skill. Through the prescribed disciplines of kenjutsu each bushi learned how to deal with all other weapons in combat. Kenjutsu became an energetic educator and a compendium of martial gymnastics, a training ground for the unity of eye and hand. While teaching the judgment of combative-engagement distance (ma-ai) and opportunity (*suki*), as well as of physical and mental domination of the enemy (zanshin), kenjutsu engendered moral

*Above left: Terauchi Kenzo (facing camera) and Otake Nobutoshi of the Tenshin Shoden Katori Shinto Ryu demonstrate* kenjutsu *with* odachi. *Terauchi has evaded an attack and prepares to counterattack.*

*Above right: Oyamada Fumio of the Tenshin Shoden Katori Shinto Ryu shows flawless two-sword (nito) technique as he withdraws to adjust the ma-ai, or combative-engagement distance.*

*Terauchi Akira (left) of the Tenshin Shoden Katori Shinto Ryu uses a* kodachi *in combat with Otake Risuke, master teacher of the ryu, who uses an* odachi. *Terauchi has avoided Otake's thrust and jumps forward to deliver a wrist cut.*

*Left: The twelfth-century warrior Kajiwara Genta Kangesue, a Genji adherent, draws his sword and raises it above his head in a posture* (kamae) *showing his determination to fight to the death.*

confidence, self-reliance, and the habit of resourcefulness in combat through training against a partner (*sotai renshu*). At the same time, kenjutsu was but preparation for dying; for to die well, with valor, was as much a matter of martial pride as was victory in combat.

Kenjutsu deals primarily with the sword after it has been unsheathed, and therefore represents an attitude in every respect aggressive, both compelling and ominous. The fundamental arm for kenjutsu is the odachi; at the appropriate level of skill, however, exponents may also train with the *kodachi,* or short sword, and with two swords, usually one short and one long, in *nito* (two-sword) or *ryoto* (both-sword) fashion.

More than five thousand ryu contain kenjutsu within their curricula. The first ryu known to have developed kenjutsu is the Tenshin Shoden Katori Shinto Ryu, founded in the fifteenth century by Choiisai Izasa Ienao.

IAI-JUTSU  The classical bushi looked upon the sword as the eternal symbol of his profession. It was, as "gentleman's steel," the best friend of bravery, and, as "pitiless steel," the worst foe of treachery. In the hands of a kenshi (expert swordsman), a finely ground and polished blade both killed and cured. For the nation at

*Warrior with drawn sword*

*Otake Risuke crouches on one knee (left) in* iai-goshi, *the posture of readiness in* iai-jutsu. *From this position he leaps high into the air (center) in the action called* nukitsuke no ken. *In a split second he has unsheathed his* odachi, *executed a forward slashing thrust, and changed leg positions. At right another action is seen.*

large, the bushi's sword was the symbol of justice and martyrdom, both a creator and a destroyer.

Because the classical bushi considered his sword as something that was both universal and persistently personal, it was not merely a tool or weapon. He believed his sword to be endowed with mystic qualities, a sentient being that spoke, sang, rejoiced, or grieved as the situation dictated. The sword became an object of identification for the bushi, who always treated it with infinite affection, just as he would a loved one; for this reason he carefully chose an appropriate name for his blade. The sword was not, as is sometimes claimed, simply the bushi's soul, but rather his living soul.

*Iai-jutsu,* or sword-drawing art, made it possible for the bushi to develop the power to triumph over mere violence. This art is essentially a defensive one, dealing as it does with methods of using a sword that must be drawn from a position of rest inside its scabbard. The technical rationale of iai-jutsu permits the swordsman to respond to situations imposed upon him by an aggressor. But the criteria by which an aggressor is defined are broad, based on *kobo-ichi,* the phenomenon by which offensive and defensive actions are basically one, to be decided on at the appropriate moment by the exponent of iai-jutsu. Unlike kenjutsu, iai-jutsu is generally per-

*Armor*

formed as a solo exercise (*tandoku renshu*) and makes much of the fact that the exponent may be seated, crouching, or reclining, and thus relatively unprepared for combat.

Four stages of sword mechanics receive emphasis in iai-jutsu: the *nukitsuke*, or draw; the *kiritsuke*, or cutting action; the *chiburi*, or removal of blood from the blade; and the *noto*, or return of the blade to its scabbard. Each of these stages must be performed in an efficient manner and smoothly blended into a single unit of performance over which an unbroken state of zanshin prevails.

Exponents of iai-jutsu are traditionally required to use only a live blade, that is, one that is razor sharp; for unless an actual sword is used, it is impossible to generate the mental attitude necessary to the art. Thus, when correctly done, the mechanics of iai-jutsu bring the exponent within fractions of an inch of the sharp blade, making the performance a literal flirt with death that must be repeated a substantial number of times daily if it is ever to be expertly performed and maintained. This threat of danger is constant whether the

*Warrior making
a spear thrust*

*Otake Risuke, armed with a spear, thrusts at the advancing leg of Otake Nobutoshi. The latter, armed with an* odachi, *is trying to reduce the* ma-ai *to be able to use his sword effectively.*

*Mori Rammaru, spear in hand, defends his master, Oda Nobunaga, against assassins sent by Akechi Mitsuhide. One enemy warrior grasps the shaft of Rammaru's spear and is pulled to his feet as Rammaru withdraws the weapon.*

trainee practices with the odachi, as is usually the case, or with the shorter blade, the kodachi.

More than four hundred ryu consider iai-jutsu within their curricula. As with kenjutsu, the Tenshin Shoden Katori Shinto Ryu developed the first iai-jutsu that can be historically verified.

SOJUTSU Japanese mythology recounts the formation of the Japanese archipelago by two divine beings, who use a spear to accomplish this feat. Thus the elemental importance of the spear to the Japanese people in general is illustrated, and the fact that the spear was among the earliest weapons to be used on the battlefield becomes understandable.

The prototypes for the Japanese warrior's *yari,* or spear, had been brought to Japanese soil from the Asian continent. None of them appears to have been entirely satisfactory to the classical bushi. The continental spearhead was a hollow globe; a shaft was fitted into it like a hand in a glove. This weapon would on occasion, through the force of the thrust and withdrawal, leave its bladed head in the victim's body. Thus, when metallurgy and weapons technology permitted, the classical bushi designed a spearhead that was fitted to its shaft by means of a long tang inserted into the shaft and held fast by multiple cord bindings wound around the shaft. It was this type

*Warrior with grappling hook*

of spearhead that was mounted on the standard Japanese weapon.

Though it was capable of great combative effect, the spear never became universally popular with the classical warrior, for the length and weight of the weapon were not ideally suited to his stature and strength. It was usually the rugged-individualist type of warrior who made the spear his special weapon. The spear enjoyed its greatest popularity after the Mongol invasions of the late thirteenth century, when the role of the foot warrior became increasingly important.

*Sojutsu*, or spear art, was looked upon as being an arrogant art, essentially the craft of the ruthless individual, for the wound produced by this weapon often inflicted a cruel and lingering death. Sojutsu trained the bushi to think of the spear more as a weapon of opportunity than as one for general tactical employment. The spear could be employed either from horseback or from the ground. Elaborate spearhead designs that included additional blade surfaces took the straight-bladed head out of the category of piercing weapons and gave it new roles in slashing, hooking, and ripping. Yet the basic mechanics of sojutsu continued unchanged, and the bushi trained primarily to be accurate with the *tsuki,* or thrust. The classical warrior, training with the spear, learned the necessity of the long ma-ai (combative-engagement distance) to bring the target within the lethal range of the point; conversely, in this process he developed an uncanny ability for avoiding the long ma-ai when facing a spearman while armed with his basic weapon, the sword.

Some four hundred fifty ryu found it necessary to include sojutsu within their teachings. Again, the Tenshin Shoden Katori Shinto Ryu lays claim to being the first historically proved source of sojutsu.

*Halberd-armed warriors*

NAGINATA-JUTSU  Early Japanese contacts with the Chinese may have resulted in the idea for the design of a halberdlike weapon. The first Japanese manufacture of this kind of weapon coincided with the emergence of the professional warrior class.

Essentially, the halberd is a man's weapon, a fact dictated by its length and weight. The earliest types were seven feet or more in length, with weights varying in proportion to the amounts of wood and metal in them. The *nagamaki* appeared first. This consisted of a

*Terauchi Kenzo jumps in* karasu-tobi, *or crow-hopping, fashion as he slashes downward with his* naginata *at retreating swordsman Otake Risuke.*

*The twelfth-century warrior-monk Musashibo Benkei, armed with his customary* naginata, *dispatches an enemy in continental Asian garb and armed with a Chinese spear.*

*Girl armed with* naginata,
*from a twelfth-century scene*

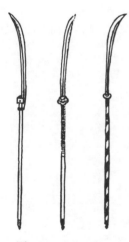

*Three types of halberd:
from left, naginata,
nagamaki, naginata*

long blade and short shaft; the bladed portion of this weapon was
not unlike a huge, heavy, curved, single-edged sword in shape. The
*naginata* differed from the nagamaki in the proportion of blade to
shaft; the shaft was always considerably longer than the blade. Like
the spearhead, the blade of both the nagamaki and the naginata was
fixed to a hardwood shaft by means of a long tang that was inserted
into the shaft and bound fast by cord wrapped around the shaft.

The nagamaki and naginata were early favorites with the bushi.
Characteristically wielded in sweeping arcs, both could be utilized
either mounted or on the ground; frequently the nagamaki was used
to sever the legs of enemy mounts. During the conflict between the
Taira and the Minamoto clans in the twelfth century, both the
nagamaki and the naginata proved their lethal effect, and when the
Mongols struck at Japan about a century later, the bushi accounted
for a substantial number of invaders by means of these vicious blades.
Later, when horses became scarce, the role of the foot warrior grew
in importance, and the keen-edged odachi was undisputedly the
warrior's most useful weapon, the nagamaki and naginata were
reduced to weapons of opportunity.

Coming under Tokugawa rule in the beginning of the seventeenth century, Japan rested in peace compared to the turbulent era that had just ended. The nagamaki and naginata then became symbols of that past. But the latter weapon, which had been used to train the women of the classical bushi, was now redesigned and given over almost entirely to women to be used as an instrument for the enrichment of their otherwise sedentary lives.

*Naginata-jutsu,* or halberd art, requires great stamina. This long heavy weapon, like the nagamaki, is employed in direct and reversal fashion, interchangeably, as the exponent makes judicious use of the blade, the shaft, and the butt. Skill in *ha-kaeshi,* the ability to change the position of the blade rapidly, enabled the warrior to slash or cut much as he would with his sword, but with the added advantage of doing so at a longer range due to the length of the shaft. An attack could be launched against a swordsman while the exponent, armed with the naginata, remained insulated by distance from the swordsman's blade. Because of this the exponent had to be expertly skilled in swordsmanship prior to undertaking training with the naginata, for defenses against the sword depended in the main on anticipation of an attacking swordsman's capabilities.

Four hundred twenty-five ryu concerned themselves with naginata-jutsu. The oldest historic claim to the pioneer effort belongs again to the Tenshin Shoden Katori Shinto Ryu.

So-hei, *warrior-monks, escorting a sacred palanquin*

# CHAPTER FIVE

# STAFF AND STICK WEAPONS

And tho' not sword, yet cudgel proff,
Whereby 'twas fitter for his use
Who fear'd no blows but such as bruise.

James Butler

BOJUTSU Wooden weapons of varying lengths have been both ceremonially and combatively used by the Japanese people since earliest times. Even Japanese mythology cites examples in which the staff served as the instrument of defensive authority. Nature has blessed the Japanese islands with an excellent hardwood called *kashi,* a type of evergreen oak, which makes a staff or stick that is all but indestructible in hand-to-hand combat.

The staff never received the plaudits of the classical bushi because it was far too humble a weapon; the lowliest person could make one. Compared to the magnificent sword, the wooden staff lacked prestige. But because of its obvious effectiveness the classical bushi could not afford to neglect its study.

Systematic combative use of the staff is known as *bojutsu,* or staff art, and makes use of a hardwood weapon, the *bo,* that measures five or more feet in length. The standard staff weapon for the bushi was the *rokushaku-bo* (six-foot staff). As a defensive art, bojutsu centers on the tactics by which an aggressive swordsman can be subdued, but other weapons can also be dealt with effectively. Methods of striking, blocking, parrying, thrusting, and covering comprise the bojutsu repertoire. The *gyakute-uchi,* a kind of reverse-grip striking action, is the basic striking technique that all exponents of bojutsu

*Two staff weapons,*
kiribo *(left)*
*and* hakkaku-bo

must master. One blow from the staff in this fashion is powerful enough to break a metal sword and to shatter bones.

Through intensive training in bojutsu the warrior learned a deep appreciation for the maintenance of optimal ma-ai, for should a swordsman be able to shorten that distance appreciably, the staff becomes ineffective.

More than three hundred ryu included bojutsu in their teachings. Again the pioneer effort must be credited to the Tenshin Shoden Katori Shinto Ryu.

JOJUTSU   One very determined fighting man's obsession brought about the development of the systematic use in combat of the fighting stick, a shorter length of hardwood than the staff. Muso Gonnosuke, a classical warrior trained in the basic Tenshin Shoden Katori Shinto Ryu teachings, desired to erase the humiliation of the defeat he had received at the hands of the famed Miyamoto Musashi, Japan's most skillful seventeenth-century swordsman.

Gonnosuke's development was *jojutsu,* or stick art. This is actually a synthesis of the characteristic actions produced by other weapons in the classical bushi's arsenal. Jojutsu makes use of the *jo,* a stick less than five feet in length, to accomplish the thrust (tsuki) of the spear, the strike (*utsu*) of the sword and staff, and the sweep (*harai*) of the naginata. These actions, when combined in a series of fast movements, are effective in defense against an aggressor armed with any standard weapon of the bujutsu.

*Two staff weapons,*
yoribo *(left)*
*and* tetsubo

Because the stick is shorter and far lighter than the staff, the techniques comprising jojutsu are quite different from those subsumed by bojutsu. One notable characteristic of jojutsu, somewhat lacking in bojutsu, is the speed and high frequency of reversals of the weapon in meeting a combative situation. The stick thus offers the exponent an excellent way to develop dexterity.

The Shindo Muso Ryu, founded in the seventeenth century, was the mother tradition for the more than seventy different styles of jojutsu that developed.

TETSUBO-JUTSU   One of the early weapons transferred from the Asian continent to Japan was the solid iron bar, a stafflike instru-

Above: Shimizu Takaji (foreground), headmaster of the Shindo Muso Ryu, armed with a hardwood stick (jo), demonstrates jojutsu as he intercepts the attack of swordsman Kuroda Ichitaro.

Below: Terauchi Akira delivers an upward strike with the bo, or hardwood staff, at defending swordsman Otake Risuke. Terauchi's leap increases the impact of the staff; the speed of the action is seen by the blur of the swordsman's blade as it moves to block the staff.

Center: Musashibo Benkei beats his master, Yoshitsune, with a heavy staff to fool the authorities into letting them pass a barrier checkpoint. In the background at left are the mitsu-dogu, the three traditional weapons of restraint.

*Combat with staff and halberd*

*Right:* The thirteenth-century warrior Asahira Saburo Yoshihide wields a konsaibo—*a variant of the* tetsubo—*as he smashes his way into an enemy stronghold.*

*Below:* Sixteenth-century warrior Honda Heihachiro Tadakatsu swings a tetsubo against his mounted opponent, Mangara Jurozaemon Naotaka.

ment. It was of various shapes and lengths, with circular, hexagonal, or octagonal cross sections. The bar normally tapered from its largest dimension, at its fore end, to a narrow handle; this facilitated gripping and also improved the weapon's balance. This cumbersome instrument had limited uses but became important as a secondary weapon with the emergence of the professional warrior class.

The general type of this weapon was known as a *tetsubo,* or iron staff. The technique of using the tetsubo was known as *tetsubo-jutsu,* or iron-staff art. Since the great weight of this formidable weapon was an unavoidable feature, only the physically strongest warriors became proficient in its use. It could be employed from either a mounted or a ground position. A lighter version of the tetsubo was the *konsaibo,* a hardwood staff reinforced by metal strips and often studded with heavy iron nubs along its upper portion.

Tetsubo-jutsu utilizes the tremendous momentum generated by the bar as it is swung or jabbed in various trajectories. Upon impact it wreaks havoc on its target. A mounted warrior armed with this weapon could confidently ride into a mass engagement, for he had tremendous odds in his favor. He had only to time the trajectory of his swing with the tetsubo to coincide with his *kurai dori* (critical approach) against the enemy, for the tetsubo bludgeoned its victims with crushing force. Use of the tetsubo on the ground required the warrior to swing the weapon with great rapidity in order to avoid weaknesses (*suki*) in his defense. When swung against the legs of horses, the tetsubo toppled mounted warriors from their saddles; then, on the ground, they could be easily dealt with. At other times the tetsubo served as a portable battering ram and could demolish entrances and strongpoints of an enemy's fortified position.

It is not known which if any of the martial traditions formalized the use of the tetsubo; perhaps they left the use of that weapon to those warriors who were sufficiently powerful to wield it.

*Combat with staffs*

# CHAPTER SIX

# ARCHERY

A good archer is not known by his arrows
but his aim.

Thomas Fuller

The bow and arrow, serving as both a weapon and an instrument
of ceremony, is referred to in the earliest extant annals of Japan,
wherein it is assigned a mythological background. Most of the
early uses of the bow and arrow in Japan centered on ceremonial
functions, but by the time of the rise of the professional warrior
class the bow had become a primary weapon of war. Two major
traditions arose, one specializing in mounted uses of the bow and
the other in ground uses.

Though continental Asian influences may be seen in the ceremonial use of the bow and arrow, the design of the Japanese bow seems
to be indigenous. The bow is asymmetrical; two-thirds of its length
towers above the bowman as he prepares to release his arrow. This
design was instituted to permit what amounts to a longbow technique from a mounted position, as a substantial amount of combat
in early Japan was conducted on horseback.

*Kyujutsu,* or bow art, had for its primary purpose the preparation
of the warrior as an accurate marksman in combat. Such skill lay not
only in physical mastery of technique but in a balanced blend of both
mental and physical qualities. In its earliest forms, kyujutsu was an
aggressive martial art. But as the role of the bowman lessened in
importance, due first to the predominance of close-quarter combat
and later to the introduction of firearms, the practical value of
kyujutsu became more defensive. Nevertheless, the disciplinary
value of kyujutsu remained, and it continued to be an important
way of nurturing and maintaining spiritual development.

*Three types of bow*

*Ogasawara Kiyonobu, headmaster of the Ogasawara Ryu,
raises and draws his bow. He is using a nari-kaburaya,
or hunming-bulb arrow, used to open combat.*

*Three types of arrow*

The first essential in kyujutsu is for the warrior to become
accomplished in the *yugamae,* or correct shooting posture, without
which the bow cannot be used efficiently. Though mounted and
unmounted shooting postures naturally differ somewhat, they are
founded on common principles. Both are designed to foster and
reflect the shooter's physical and mental dominance (zanshin) over
his enemy. That state of dominance must continue even after the
arrow has been released. In training, the warrior shot thousands of
arrows over a range of only a few feet into a specially prepared
target. Only when his shooting form was correct did he attempt to

*The tenth-century warrior Taira Sadamori, governor of Hitachi Province, aims an arrow at the rebel chieftain Taira Masakado, who carries a* tetsubo.

extend his skill over longer distances. The *inagashi* (flight) shooting method was the supreme test of the unmounted bowman. In this kind of shooting he was required to sustain a volley of arrows for hours on end; this was useful in interdicting an enemy's position. Mounted bowmen found their supreme test in the *yabusame*, a sacred ritual that involved shooting at targets while riding at a full gallop.

Historically speaking, the Nihon Ryu was the pioneer in kyu-jutsu. By the fifteenth century it had stimulated the establishment of six other major ryu.

*Two types of quiver*

# CHAPTER SEVEN

# COMPOSITE WEAPONS

Grant a combat with us:
We are two, you are seven.
No matter!

Trautman

NINJUTSU  The need for effective espionage was recognized early by Japanese fighting men. Ability to gather intelligence about an enemy or potential enemy was an indispensable part of their profession. Espionage was conducted as a preliminary to battlefield engagement, and though it was a concomitant feature of all ages of Japanese warriors, espionage in a highly developed and systematic form was the product of the age when the classical warriors ruled the land.

Eventually the art of martial espionage was termed *ninjutsu,* or the art of stealing in; its exponents were called *ninja,* "stealers in." Ninja were not of the aristocratic bushi class but of a particularly low social level known as *hinin* (literally, "not human"). When captured by bushi, ninja were subjected to the most undignified deaths. At the same time, ninja were hired by bushi to perform necessary acts of espionage. So varied and spectacular did the daring deeds of the ninja become that many bushi themselves used ninjutsu techniques in their own operations. No leader of bushi could afford to be without an efficient network of spies, and because of this constant need he usually augmented his ninja with bushi trained in ninjutsu. This served still another important purpose. Ninja were susceptible to bribes, which led them to commit treason or other treacherous

*Crest of the Iga
ninjutsu* ryu

acts on behalf of anyone who bid higher than their original master.

The bushi generally took an extremely practical view of their martial studies, all learning being geared for efficient combative application. However, ninjutsu, being a composite skill and derived from various sources, was not without a strong element of superstition. Through ninjutsu, certain occult beliefs and practices were carried to the bushi and thus affected the bujutsu.

Aside from the fantastic feats of agility, speed, and endurance, as well as the resourceful fighting skills included in ninjutsu training, the bushi learned other important matters. He discovered how to compound medicine: antiseptic balms, lotions, and first-aid remedies to be applied to wounds to eliminate infection and promote healing could be made from common plants and other substances. A particular compound imbibed with tea before retiring served to awaken the bushi when danger lurked nearby. Other compounds were highly toxic agents to be used against enemies.

Certain tactical advantages were derived from the ninja's knowledge of woodsmanship. Rising birds warned of a hidden enemy; in their flight, birds always rise toward uninhabited areas. The sounds of crickets, cicadas, certain other insects, and frogs told of the absence of human beings; when such noises suddenly stopped, a stealthy intruder was in the area. The bushi even learned to be aware of extra-heavy humming from mosquitoes, which might be evidence of a human nearby. Disguise was also important to the bushi. The role of the *komuso* (beggar-ascetic), much favored by the ninja, became a standard disguise for the bushi, as well. Camouflage, arson, codes, and signaling techniques, too, were in part borrowed from the ninja. The preparation of fire bombs, fire arrows, and smoke screens were still other bits of knowledge that the bushi learned through his contacts with ninja. When a bushi had need to bolster his courage he relied on Buddhist occult lore, conditioned by the *kuji-kiri* (nine-symbols cutting), the esoteric hand signs employed by the ninja and believed to have magical power.

Not all ryu found it necessary to formalize a ninjutsu tradition of their own. On the basis of historical evidence, the Tenshin Shoden Katori Shinto Ryu was the first to do so.

*Crest of the Koga ninjutsu* ryu

Kusarigama *expert Shimizu Takaji, headmaster of the Isshin Ryu, releases the weighted chain of his weapon (left) against swordsman Kaminoda Tsunemori, ensnaring him (center). Then, having parried*

KUSARIGAMA-JUTSU A hand-held sickle used as a weapon is a very old idea. In Japan, its use as a weapon was encouraged by the fact that the early agricultural settlers employed the sickle to reap grain. With the establishment of the professional warrior class, various innovations in the design of the sickle were introduced, and by the end of the fifteenth century a sicklelike weapon to which a weighted chain was attached, known as the *kusarigama,* was in use.

Two distinct types of kusarigama exist. One is a farmer's weapon, the other a warrior's weapon. The former is characterized by a rather short blade, shaped somewhat like a parrot's beak, attached to a hardwood handle. The warrior's type is actually a short sword hafted onto a hardwood handle. A weighted chain is common to both types of kusarigama, though the pattern of linkage and the suspension of the chain differ. The farmer's type of weapon has neither the cast range nor the lethal effect in close-quarter fighting of the warrior's weapon.

The kusarigama is several weapons in one. It is at once a bladed weapon, a stick or club weapon, and a flail. *Kusarigama-jutsu,* or chain and sickle art, is a corpus of defensive techniques with many interesting ramifications. The user of the warrior's kusarigama can slash or cut the enemy with the razor-sharp double-edged blade; skewer him with the point of the blade; ensnare and painfully

*Warrior armed
with sickle
and swords*

*a sword thrust by Kaminoda, Shimizu strikes at his neck with the sickle portion of the* kusarigama.
*(Photos by James S. Ogata)*

constrict him or render his weapon useless by means of the tough, uncuttable iron chain; break his bones through the momentum generated by the iron weight at the end of the chain; or club him senseless with the hardwood handle.

Expert skill with the kusarigama is developed only after thousands of hours of training experience. The prime necessity is perfection of the *maki,* the ensnaring action of the chain against the enemy's weapon. Such a skill requires the exponent to come within a hairbreadth of the enemy's attack, such as coming in close under an overhead and downward descent of a sword blade. Thus judgment of the ma-ai is of critical importance because the slightest error can result in death. Yet apart from such delicate moments, every advantage lies on the side of the warrior-expert using the kusarigama because of the diversity of this weapon's application.

Most warriors considered the kusarigama a specialty weapon, and many thought it unfair because of its composite nature. Perhaps the length of time required to become expert in its use was the greatest factor limiting its popularity.

Kusarigama

About one hundred ryu made use of the kusarigama, the pioneer effort, on the basis of historical evidence, being credited to the Isshin Ryu, founded in the fifteenth century by a monk named Jion.

*Using a sickle as a weapon*

TESSEN-JUTSU   The classical warrior overlooked no object that might be used as a weapon. Thus the ordinary folding fan, seemingly the most innocent of objects, provided at least some of the inspiration for the development of the *tessen,* or iron fan.

There were moments in the daily life of the warrior in which he was, at least to outward appearances, largely defenseless. When engaged in domestic chores, when at leisure, or when attending the social occasions required of him in dealings with his superiors and colleagues, the warrior was bound by certain formalities that limited his capacity to fight effectively. Under certain conditions the warrior might be required to leave one or both of his swords with an attendant of his host. But armed with the tessen, which he wore thrust through his sash, he was, in fact, never completely unarmed. Should an emergency arise, the warrior could easily defend himself with what otherwise appeared to be a harmless and common article of personal wear.

Two types of tessen were developed: the kind that could be opened, much like the ordinary fan, and the kind that was an unopenable solid in the shape of a closed fan. But the feature of durability was common to both types. Generally, the principal

*The herculean warrior-monk Musashibo Benkei uses a* kusarigama *in descending a cliff.*

*The fourteenth-century warrior Kusunoki Masashige, tessen in hand, directs a battle against Ashikaga rebels. Jumping into the fray below is warrior-monk Honshobo Enjuku.*

material used in the construction of the tessen was iron. In the case of the variety that could be opened, the ribs of the fan were made of iron, while the material covering them was a special kind of paper on which some design was drawn, usually a family crest or a decorative design. The solid tessen was the more durable and proved to be the more popular type. Hardwood was sometimes substituted for iron to lighten the weapon and to make maintenance easier.

The nature of the tessen, however constructed, when used as a weapon is primarily that of a secondary, defensive device. In a strict technical sense, the manner of fighting with a tessen is related to the techniques of short-stick manipulation, from which much of the application of the tessen arises. It is of fundamental importance to the bearer of a tessen to select the proper *sashikata* (way of wearing the tessen in one's sash); it must be positioned so as to be instantly available. Tactics involving the use of the tessen revolve largely around those of blocking (*uke*), parrying (*nagashi*), holding (*osae*), striking (*uchi*), and thrusting (*tsuki*). The effect of the tessen is strengthened when it is employed in conjunction with some other weapon. Used with the kodachi, the tactic of *juji-dome* (cross-block) was particularly effective. This could render an enemy's weapon inoperable for a fraction of a second, during which the defender was already delivering his counterattack.

Slightly more than one hundred traditions formalized the use of the tessen. On the basis of historical evidence the Shinkage Ryu, founded in the sixteenth century, must be credited with the first systematization.

*A troop commander holding a tessen*

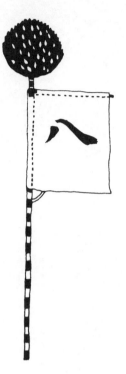

CHAPTER EIGHT

# GRAPPLING

Fiercely stand,
or fighting fall.

Byron

YOROI KUMI-UCHI Grappling methods used for combat are as
old as man on the Asian continent; and this is no less true in Japan.
Japanese mythology recounts grappling combats between deities to
determine divine authority for leadership of the land. In the ninth
century A.D. primitive grappling methods came under the purview
of the warrior class. Later, when warriors dominated Japan, such
grappling skills became the foundation for improved systems of
fighting at close quarters between adversaries who were fully clad
in armor.

Methods of grappling dominated the close-quarter-combat systems of the warriors simply because those of a purely kick-and-
strike nature proved ineffective against weapons and armor. No
classical warrior was without skill in grappling.

*Yoroi kumi-uchi,* or grappling in armor, is a practical system of
combat that became necessary when warriors engaged in single
combat abandoned, for whatever reason, their major weapons. But
yoroi kumi-uchi combat is not necessarily unarmed combat. No
combative system of the classical bujutsu requires the warrior to be
unarmed, though included are methods of fighting while only
minimally armed. One of the most useful weapons for yoroi kumi-
uchi is the short blade, such as the kodachi.

Yoroi kumi-uchi requires the combatants to use their hips and
limbs in a peculiar, powerful fashion. This is made possible through
the *yotsu-gumi,* a four-handed symmetrical method of gripping by
which the combatants lock to each other without actually grasping

*The drawings of* yoroi kumi-uchi *on this and the facing page are from a manual of the Genkai Ryu.*

the armor. Mastering the yotsu-gumi was essential to effective grappling in armor; through this manner of lockup the warrior developed the balance, leverage, and mobility with which both to preserve his position and to hurl his enemy to the ground. At any appropriate moment in the standing grappling action, either warrior could draw his short blade and attempt to plunge it into his adversary. A special blade, the *yoroi-doshi,* was worn thrust through a sash at the right hip for this purpose; it was usually drawn left-handed. But of course great skill was required to maintain one's own balance and control the struggles of the enemy while one hand sought to unsheathe the short blade and plunge it into a vital point on his body. In addition, to insinuate the blade between the sections of the foe's armor at the proper angle was extremely difficult.

A large number of classical combative traditions gave considerable attention to the study of yoroi kumi-uchi. On the basis of historical evidence the Tsutsumi-hozan Ryu, a fifteenth-century martial tradition, appears to have been the first to do so.

*Two experts of the Yagyu Shingan Ryu demonstrate* yoroi kumi-uchi, *grappling in armor. The man in the foreground has unbalanced his opponent, who is preparing to plunge his armor-piercing dagger,* yoroi-doshi, *into the other's chest. (Photo courtesy of Rekishi Dokuhon)*

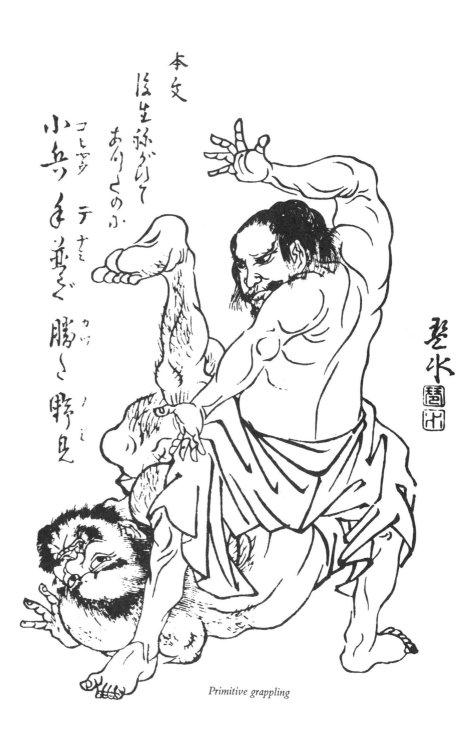

本文

後生弥がりて
ありくのふ

コヒャウ テさ

小兵手をぎ 勝と野見

*Primitive grappling*

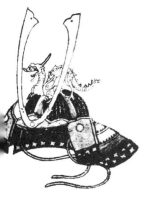

*Warrior's helmet*

*Kato Kiyomasa prepares to bind Shihoden Sashima in* hojo-jutsu *fashion after subduing him by* yoroi kumi-uchi *grappling.*

HOJO-JUTSU In yoroi kumi-uchi, as well as other forms of grappling, the victor did not necessarily wish to kill his victim. Under certain circumstances it was desirable to take the foe alive. Thus, closely allied to close-quarter grappling methods were systems of tying an adversary so that he could not escape.

Methods of binding an enemy did not consist solely of wrapping layers of cord around the victim in haphazard fashion, however secure those methods might be. In the compartmentalized social structure of protofeudal and feudal Japan, great care was taken to apply certain patterns of binding to each social class. But recognition of the victim's social status was a minor reason for this custom.

The costumes, tools, weapons, personal habits, and skills of each social class differed, and these factors played a decisive role in the manner in which different people were tied. The noble, the warrior, the farmer, the merchant, the artisan, the monk, and the beggar were each tied in a different way. Anatomical differences between male and female also led the warriors to devise different methods of binding men and women.

*Hojo-jutsu,* or cord-tying art, comprises all methods used to tie and immobilize a victim by means of cord after the victim has been subdued by some combative means. The warrior was trained to develop *te no uchi,* the finesse of hand that alone can guarantee efficient tying. Simply trussing the victim securely was not the only requirement of hojo-jutsu. Tying had to be done quickly, often while the victim was still struggling to escape. Thus hojo-jutsu operated as an important secondary system within the bujutsu, fully dependent upon the warrior's skill in capturing and controlling his foe by grappling methods. The special cord used in hojo-jutsu was normally carried by all warriors as part of their battle equipment. But often a field expedient was used when the warrior found himself with nothing more than his *sageo,* the short length of cord attached to the scabbard of his odachi, with which to bind an enemy. Properly trained, the warrior could still immobilize his victim with amazing efficiency.

Few classical combative traditions ignored the study of hojo-jutsu. Historically speaking, the Takenouchi Ryu was the first to formalize methods of tying.

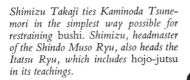

*Shimizu Takaji ties Kaminoda Tsunemori in the simplest way possible for restraining bushi. Shimizu, headmaster of the Shindo Muso Ryu, also heads the Itatsu Ryu, which includes hojo-jutsu in its teachings.*

CHAPTER NINE

# AUXILIARY ARTS

The combat deepens,
On ye brave
Who rush to glory or
The grave.

Thomas Campbell

BAJUTSU Skeletal remains found in Japan indicate that the horse existed there in prehistoric times, a fact that Japanese mythology corroborates. Even before the professional warrior class had been established, mounted fighting men roamed the country. Later, as the classical warrior rose to decide the political issues that had divided the country, horsemanship was an inseparable part of his martial curriculum. He who possessed a suitable mount gave visual evidence of his aristocratic background, and this element of prestige was an important factor in assuming leadership over other warriors.

During the Kamakura period the daily routine of the classical warrior reflected his profession at arms. He was under constant martial discipline, and much of his time was necessarily taken up with the practice of *bajutsu,* or horse art. By means of the horse the bushi was able to use his weapons more effectively, in particular the bow and arrow, sword, spear, and nagamaki or naginata. The need to ford streams and cross other bodies of water also led to the development of a branch of horsemanship known as *sui-bajutsu,* or water horse-art.

Though each bushi might accept the fact that it was his sword, not his horse, that generally saved the day for him in combat, nevertheless he devoted meticulous attention to *kihon,* or fundamentals, of riding. *Norikata,* or the correct manner of mounting, preceded all other training. Once in the saddle, the bushi knew the urgency of developing the loin strength to maintain for hours on end the posture necessary for swift riding. And development of a seat that would provide a stable base from which to ride without holding the reins as he wielded his major weapons was an absolute condition of his profession.

On the basis of historical records, the fifteenth-century Otsubo Ryu first systematized bajutsu; this led to the development of more than fifty different traditions.

*Mounted warriors*

*Akisaka Jinnai, riding a black charger and armed with a spear, uses his horse to edge his
enemy Kondo Takeichi over the edge of a cliff during the battle of Shizugatake in 1583.*

*Higuchi Sadahiro, headmaster of the Maniwa Nen Ryu, displays perfect timing as he deflects an arrow with his wakizashi. He has closed his eyes to keep arrow splinters from entering them.*

*Two* yadome-jutsu *scenes*

*Various types of spear*

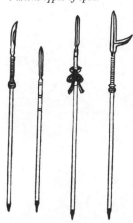

YADOME-JUTSU Fighting men who faced a deadly rain of arrows naturally sought the protection of devices behind which they could safeguard their bodies. The Japanese warriors constructed and employed large portable shields for this purpose. Their use was limited to providing cover for siege missions, for warriors in assembly areas, and during predeployment approaches, regrouping, and similar tactical dispositions. The Japanese warrior carried no buckler in battle; this was regarded as the device of a coward, in addition to which the techniques of wielding the warrior's major weapons made the use of a hand-held shield impractical.

Though the warrior carried no special device for protecting himself from volleys of arrows once he was deployed, field expedients were utilized for this purpose. The first of these was the warrior's *kabuto* (helmet). Carried in the left hand, the helmet was positioned in front of the body, and by means of deft manipulation a warrior might deflect arrows intended for him. But a far more common expedient involved the use of the warrior's sword. Using either a

*The sixteenth-century warrior Yushisama no Suke rides his charger into a swift-flowing river to escape Yasato Kyutaro, who is about to follow him into the current.*

single blade or two blades, the warrior calmly faced his enemy and blocked or deflected arrows with the blade or blades.

*Yadome-jutsu,* or arrow-stopping art, became an important part of the martial curriculum of the classical warrior. Training in yadome-jutsu developed sharpness of eye, super-quick reflexes, and the utmost self-confidence. Of critical importance was the *kamae,* or combative engagement posture, which had to be correct if the warrior was safely to deflect arrows in midflight. An unerring ability to judge ma-ai was likewise essential. The degree of difficulty in deflecting speeding arrows varied inversely with the distance between the target and the bowman. Zanshin was at its peak in yadome-jutsu, for the slightest mistake in posture and concentration could result in death. Arrows that approached but never threatened the body, no matter how close they came, were to be ignored; only those arrows coming directly at him received the warrior's attention.

One of the first traditions to formalize yadome-jutsu was the seventeenth-century Maniwa Nen Ryu.

*Various types of spear*

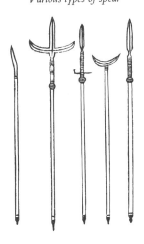

*Ceremonial spears*

*Two warriors continue their mortal combat even under water; Imanari Rikinosuke straddles Shimitsu Konai and readies his kodachi to take the other's head.*

SUIEI-JUTSU  Primitive man overcame his natural fear of water by devising means of floating and swimming. Experience with water was an accepted part of early Japanese life; Japan is surrounded by seas, and in all areas there are many rivers, streams, lakes, and ponds. Mention is made in Japanese mythology of swimming, and the early Japanese fighting man found it to his advantage to be able to swim. Thus, with the appearance of the warrior class, combative swimming became a highly developed art.

Topographical differences affecting the depths and currents of rivers and the sea gave rise to distinctly different styles of swimming among warriors. Surface swimming as well as underwater techniques developed because of differences in water depth; fast-moving and meandering bodies of water dictated still other technical peculiarities in swimming.

Combative swimming served various purposes: it enabled a warrior to swim silently while approaching the enemy, and it allowed him to stay afloat for long periods. Through skill in swimming, the warrior was able to cross a strong current or swim against it; to swim while fully clad in armor; to carry banners or flags, weapons, and heavy burdens; and to use his bow or firearms while almost completely submerged. The warrior also devised methods of grappling while in the water; he even practiced ways to overcome an enemy by grappling with him while falling from a vessel to the water. Other styles of combative swimming enabled the warrior to disentangle himself from water plants and seaweed that impeded his arms and legs, to get out of whirlpools or eddy currents, and even to jump out of the water into boats.

*Suiei-jutsu,* or swimming art, is composed of fundamentals, such as the *fumi-ashi,* or treading-water, action that is the basis of many of a warrior's combative skills in the water. Special skills like the *inatobi,* "jumping like a mullet," enabled the warrior to leap from the water. The *ashi-garami,* a technique of grappling in water, permitted the warrior to entwine an enemy's leg with sufficient force to cause him to submit or drown. And the secret method of the *shusoku-garami* enabled him to swim even when his arms and legs were bound. Few classical warriors could afford to neglect combative swimming.

The sixteenth-century Shinden Ryu has the earliest historically proven claim to being the first martial tradition to formalize combative swimming.

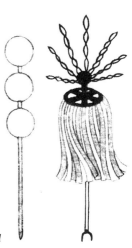

*Two types of standard*

# CLASSICAL BUJUTSU TODAY

Even though the classical bujutsu was created in and for a special segment of feudal Japanese society, it is a mistake to conclude that its disciplines are outdated or are meant only for the Japanese people. Today, in the twentieth century, many ryu of the classical bujutsu continue to function. In their modern roles these ryu constitute a cultural reservoir of beliefs, customs, and practices that exert a beneficial influence on modern man in his quest for ways of improving his relationships with his fellow men.

One of the main reasons the classical ryu have been able to maintain their extraordinary elastic vigor over the long course of their history is that they are always very much concerned with the *naka-ima,* the "middle-now," or "eternal present." Thus, in spite of the turbulent and powerful forces of time that inevitably seek to erode all things, the classical martial disciplines have changed very little, either in purpose or form, from their original nature. But there are certain important points that must be understood by those who are attracted to the classical martial disciplines and who desire to participate in them.

The classical bujutsu are unapproachable by the masses, Japanese and non-Japanese alike, for the simple reason that the men who are in positions of authority within the ryu are guided by the criterion of quality, not quantity, in choosing among the candidates who make applications for membership. By and large the members of the classical ryu display an inborn sense of duty, as well as a strong feeling of genuine brotherhood closely akin to that within a family. They further possess a dominant attitude of mind in which service to the past is regarded both as an act of gratitude to the present and

*Charter of the Tenshin Shoden Katori Shinto Ryu, oldest extant classical bujutsu ryu*

also as a sense of responsibility for what will develop in the future.

All modern exponents of the classical bujutsu stand firm in their conviction that the personal satisfactions they derive from their chosen way of life are applicable to the conditions of modern-day living, with no need to make changes in the disciplines that they practice. Necessarily, then, they are conservative men who exercise a great resistance to changes imposed by the force of fashion; they accomplish this by isolating their ryu from the contagion of ideas that are contrary to the values and norms of the classical warrior. The modern exponent is unshakable in his belief that it is worthwhile for man in any age to make use of specialized skills for the achievement of self-discipline, to develop self-respect by adherence to a code of honor, to live an unsophisticated way of life in order to gain and maintain sound mental and physical health, and to foster a sense of cooperation with other members of society.

A candidate for admission to a classical bujutsu ryu must understand that gaining membership in a ryu is actually a manner of establishing contact with an important aspect of the Japanese

*Kneeling warrior*

*Kashima Jingu, located northeast of Tokyo in Ibaraki Prefecture, enshrines the spirit of Takemikazuchi-no-kami, a deity of the sword. Founded in the Heian period (794–1185), it is the tutelary shrine of the Kashima Ryu and offers special protection to arrowsmiths.*

*Takeda Shingen holding a gumbai-uchiwa war fan*

national ethos. Unless the candidate takes the interests of the ryu to heart and wholeheartedly supports them, unless he possesses and displays a deep respect for the Japanese beliefs and customs of the past, it is certain that no classical ryu will accept him.

The candidate will be expected to be both introduced and recommended to the headmaster of the ryu he seeks to enter. These are formalities that cannot be waived. They must be initiated by somebody whom the headmaster trusts implicitly. But even after the preliminary formalities have been accomplished, the candidate may be required to undergo a probationary period, during which the depth of his motivation and fitness for martial study are probed, before his membership is approved. A word here about the candidate's personal background is relevant. The modern exponents of the classical bujutsu ryu are normally descendants of some of Japan's

*Katori Jingu is located east of Tokyo in Chiba Prefecture. Also founded in the Heian period, it enshrines the spirit of Futsunushi-no-kami, a deity of the sword. It is the tutelary shrine of the Tenshin Shoden Katori Shinto Ryu and offers special protection to swordsmen and horsemen.*

most famous martial families, or *buke*. Accordingly, they place a preference on candidates who stem from similar ancestry. Candidates who are engaged in military or law-enforcement professions, because of their familiarity with discipline, are also preferred candidates. Finally, those who, whatever their ancestral origins and occupations, are in sympathy with the classical warrior's way of life are generally considered to be suitable candidates. Required of all candidates, however, are a mental makeup and outlook on life that indicate the existence of a wholesome personal character. Such personal traits as are revealed by the demonstration of virtues like courage, honor, and loyalty, as well as emotional stability, docility before authority, a sense of national honor, and a voluntary submission to rigorous discipline regularly practiced over a protracted period of time are considered necessary.

*The* mitsu-dogu

108

*Sketches of warriors training from a manual of the Genkai Ryu*

Once he has been accepted as a member of a classical ryu the novice trainee (*nyumonsha*) is expected to execute a blood oath (*keppan*) before he can begin his study. The focus of all initial training lies in severe physical exercise. Through direct, personal experience with different weapons and the methods of using them, the trainee quickly learns that the classical bujutsu are not to be talked about or dabbled in, but rather to be savored in the fullness that comes only of personal experience through action. An understanding of what he is doing rests not in thought or words, not in what can be conveyed by the intellect, but rather in the process of "taking hold," something that is managed by the trainee himself in the spontaneity of experience. In spite of the dominantly physical nature of the training, the trainee should expect to undergo a remolding of his mind that instructs him in the spirit of cooperation and tunes his intuitive processes to a new degree of acuity. The depth and thoroughness that the trainee achieves in his study of the martial arts is measurable and will be evident to him, beyond his skill with weapons techniques, in the sense of inner peace and security that comes to him with sufficient training.

The pursuance of a classical martial art is a unique challenge to any person. No matter what degree of personal satisfaction or level of technical proficiency is currently being derived from participation

*Warrior with staff*

in such modern cognate disciplines as kendo, judo, karate-do, or aiki-do, it is worthwhile that all adepts consider making a study of a true classical martial art. Nor should those who lack experience in any of the modern forms be discouraged from beginning a study of a classical martial art simply because they have had no prior experience in the modern disciplines.

Most important to all who contemplate the study of a classical bujutsu is to obtain instruction only from qualified and licensed instructors. In Japan this is a simple matter, but in the West the situation is bleak. Few qualified instructors of the classical bujutsu reside outside Japan. Unfortunately, there are also a number of people, both Japanese and non-Japanese, who claim to be instructors in classical disciplines; armed with bogus credentials they exploit the inability of the general public to identify competent and licensed teaching authorities. Then too, a person who is interested in classical martial arts can easily confuse these disciplines with their counterparts, the classical martial ways, or budo, a subject that for the sake of thoroughness must be left for discussion in a subsequent volume. To aid the interested reader in locating a recognized instructor of the classical bujutsu, the name and address of a Japanese national organization that has cognizance over all classical ryu in Japan are listed below. All queries concerning the classical disciplines should be addressed to this organization:

*Warrior with a battle standard*

Kobudo Shinkokai
3, Kojimachi 6-chome
Chiyoda-ku, Tokyo 102

Yabusame

# Glossary-Index

NOTE: Page numbers in italics indicate illustrations.

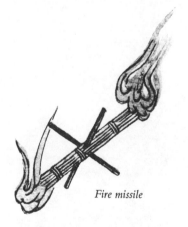

*Fire missile*

*Mounted warrior with battle-ax*

The "weathermark" identifies this book as a production of Weatherhill, Inc., publishers of fine books on Asia and the Pacific. Book design and typography by Ronald V. Bell. Cover design by D. S. Noble. Printing and binding by Quebecor Printing, Book Press. The text is set in Bembo, with Optima for display.